Back to Basics:
Keys to Spiritual Growth

Back to Basics:
Keys to Spiritual Growth

by
John MacArthur, Jr.

"GRACE TO YOU"
P.O. Box 4000
Panorama City, CA   91412

Contents

These Bible studies are taken from messages delivered by Pastor-Teacher John MacArthur, Jr., at Grace Community Church in Panorama City, California. These messages have been combined into a 6-tape album titled *Back to Basics: Keys to Spiritual Growth*. You may purchase this series either in an attractive vinyl cassette album or as individual cassettes. To purchase these tapes, request the album *Back to Basics: Keys to Spiritual Growth*, or ask for the tapes by their individual GC numbers. Please consult the current price list; then, send your order, making your check payable to:

The Master's Communication
P.O. Box 4000
Panorama City, CA 91412

Or call the following toll-free number:
1-800-55-GRACE

1
Keys to Spiritual Growth—Introduction

Outline

A. The Priority of Spiritual Growth
B. Observations About Spiritual Growth
   1. It isn't necessarily related to our position in Christ
   2. It isn't necessarily related to God's love
   3. It isn't necessarily related to time
   4. It isn't necessarily related to knowledge
   5. It isn't necessarily related to religious activity
   6. It isn't necessarily related to prosperity
C. A Definition of Spiritual Growth
D. The Master Key to Spiritual Growth
   1. The illustrations of God's glory
      a) Mankind
      b) The universe
      c) The animals
      d) The angels
   2. The responses to God's glory
      a) Change
      b) Condemnation
   3. The revelation of God's glory
      a) In the past
         (1) Adam and Eve
         (2) Moses
         (3) The cloud and pillar of fire
         (4) The Tabernacle
         (5) The Temple
         (6) Christ
      b) In the future
      c) In the present
   4. The rejection of God's glory

E. The Progression of Spiritual Growth
   1. "Little children"
   2. "Young men"
   3. "Fathers"

Introduction

A. The Priority of Spiritual Growth

Spiritual growth is one of the most important topics a believer can study in the Word of God. Two introductory verses will help put that vitally important theme in perspective:

1. 2 Peter 3:18—"Grow in grace, and in the knowledge of our Lord and Savior, Jesus Christ. To him be glory both now and forever. Amen."

2. 1 Peter 2:2—"As newborn babes, desire the pure milk of the word, that ye may grow by it."

Peter began and ended his practical epistles with an injunction for Christians to grow. Spiritual growth is essential to the life of a believer, just as physical growth is essential to the life of a child. Because God commands us to mature spiritually, we need to understand how that happens.

B. Observations About Spiritual Growth

It is important to understand several concepts that are *not* the primary issues in spiritual growth:

1. It isn't necessarily related to our position in Christ

A person doesn't grow into a Christian; conversion is an instantaneous miracle. The moment one exercises saving faith, he becomes part of the Body of Christ. Though exposure to the gospel may be a process, salvation itself is not. It is a sudden passage from death into life, "from the power of darkness . . . into the kingdom of his dear Son" (Col. 1:13).

a) 2 Corinthians 5:17—"If any man be in Christ, he is a new creation."

b) Colossians 2:10—"Ye are complete in him."

c) 2 Peter 1:3—The believer receives "all things that pertain unto life and godliness."

Each believer has received "all spiritual blessings in heavenly places in Christ" (Eph. 1:3). All the resources we need for spiritual growth are available to us.

2. It isn't necessarily related to God's love

Sometimes a parent will say to a child, "If you do what I want, I'll love you." God would never say that because He loves us no matter what we do. According to Romans 5:1-11, He loved us when we were sinners. We were His enemies, alienated from Him before we ever came to Christ. When you became a believer, God continued to love you. There are not degrees of love with God; He loves all people equally. If you are a believer, God loves you as one of His family and you cannot gain more of His love.

3. It isn't necessarily related to time

Many people saved for a long period of time have grown little, and many people saved for a brief period have grown much. The believer's commitment to growth is what matters, not the amount of time elapsed since his conversion. Spiritual maturity cannot be measured by the calendar.

4. It isn't necessarily related to knowledge

The issue is not knowledge alone but what you do with what you know. The Bible says that "knowledge puffeth up" (1 Cor. 8:1). It can make a believer prideful and can retard spiritual growth. Only when knowledge conforms us to the image of Christ does it help us grow.

5. It isn't necessarily related to religious activity

Some people think they have grown spiritually if they have served on a committee, sung in the choir, or been otherwise active in the church. They assume that if they're busy, they must be spiritual. But the Pharisees were busy with religion, and no one was further from the truth than they were. In Matthew 7:22-23 Jesus says, "Many will say to me in that day, Lord, Lord, have we not . . . done many wonderful works? And then will I profess unto them, I never knew you; depart from me." Being busy doesn't even result in salvation, let alone maturity.

6. It isn't necessarily related to prosperity

Many people equate their economic situation with favor from God. If they possess much, they think God has blessed them because they are such wonderful Christians. God may have blessed them, but that isn't necessarily an indication that they are spiritually mature.

C. A Definition of Spiritual Growth

Spiritual growth is not mystical, sentimental, devotional, or psychological. It's not the result of some clever secret or formula. It is simply matching your practice with your position. The believer's position in Christ is perfect: we are complete in Him (Col. 2:10). We have all things that pertain to life and godliness (2 Pet. 1:3). We have received all spiritual blessings (Eph. 1:3). But now we need to progress in our daily lives in a way that is commensurate with our exalted position.

D. The Master Key to Spiritual Growth

We find the most important concept in understanding and experiencing spiritual growth in 2 Peter 3:18: "Grow in grace, and in the knowledge of our Lord and Savior, Jesus Christ. To him be glory both now and forever. Amen." Giving glory to God is essentially related to spiritual growth. Therefore, it is vital that we understand what it means to glorify Him.

1. The illustrations of God's glory

   Everything exists for the purpose of glorifying God.

   a) Mankind

   The Westminster Shorter Catechism of the seventeenth century begins by stating that the chief end of man is to glorify God and enjoy Him forever.

   b) The universe

   Psalm 19:1 says, "The heavens declare the glory of God." The vastness of space and all therein glorifies God.

   c) The animals

   In Isaiah 43:20 God says, "The beast of the field shall honor me."

   d) The angels

   The angels who appeared at the birth of Christ said, "Glory to God in the highest" (Luke 2:14).

   The book of Revelation tells us that at history's climax—when God redeems His people and is ready to set up His glorious kingdom—a great song will be sung giving glory to God and the Lamb (cf. 5:8-14).

   King David said, "I have set the Lord always before me. . . . Therefore my heart is glad" (Ps. 16:8-9). David continually focused on the glory of God and received joy in return.

2. The responses to God's glory

   a) Change

   As we glorify God, we begin to grow. Second Corinthians 3:18 says, "We all, with unveiled face beholding as in a mirror the glory of the Lord, are changed into the same image from glory to glory, even as by the Spirit of the Lord." Because of the great truths revealed in the New Testament, believers can now view God's glory more clearly than those under the law could. As we do, we grow spiritually, moving from one level of glory to the next.

As the end of verse 18 says, the Holy Spirit energizes our growth. "The Spirit giveth life" (v. 6), and growth is one aspect of life. He infuses our lives with His power, taking us through levels of glory toward the image of Christ. We should not be preoccupied with the Holy Spirit's work, however, or with our own activity. We should focus primarily on the glory of the Lord.

b) Condemnation

God's judgment has fallen on the human race because of its failure to give Him glory. The apostle Paul recounts mankind's defection from the truth in Romans 1-3. In Romans 1:21, he tells us the basic problem with mankind: "When they knew God, they glorified him not as God."

All civilizations knew God through their conscience "because that which may be known of God is manifest in them" (v. 19). They also knew Him through creation, "for the invisible things of him from the creation of the world are clearly seen" (v. 20). But though men had both an internal and an external knowledge of God, they failed to give Him glory. Instead, they "changed the glory of the incorruptible God into an image made like corruptible man, and birds, and four-footed beasts, and creeping things" (v. 23). They invented idolatrous systems of religion.

When man abandoned the concept of glorifying God, he cut himself off from spiritual life and growth. The history of man is therefore a descent, not an ascent. He cannot grow because he refuses to give God glory.

12

3. The revelation of God's glory

   a) In the past

   Throughout human history, God has endeavored to show men His glory. He wants to reverse the Fall so that men will turn toward His glory rather than away from it.

   (1) Adam and Eve

   Genesis 3:8 says that Adam and Eve "heard the voice of the Lord God walking in the garden in the cool of the day." Before the Fall, Adam and Eve lived in the presence of God. Since God is a spirit (John 4:24), He probably didn't have a body in the Garden of Eden. I believe He manifested Himself in a glorious, incandescent, brilliant light. That's the way He appears elsewhere in Scripture.

   Adam and Eve had fellowship with the representation of God's infinite and eternal glory. When they sinned, however, God immediately threw them out of the Garden and cut them off from His glory. He even placed an angel with a sword at the entrance of the Garden to keep them out (Gen. 3:24). Fallen man cannot dwell in God's presence or experience His glory.

   From that tragic point in human history until today, God's purpose has been to get men to see His glory.

   (2) Moses

   In Exodus 33, the Israelites are being led by Moses. They had reached a crisis point in their life as a nation, after leaving Egypt for the Promised Land. God wanted them to know He is a God of great glory. He wanted them to see His glory, to have His presence with them, and to acknowledge Him for who He is.

(*a*) Moses' request

Some estimate that there may have been as many as two million people in the camp. Although he had been commissioned by God to lead Israel into the Promised Land, Moses was afraid because of his inabilities and said, "See, thou sayest unto me, Bring up this people: and thou hast not let me know whom thou wilt send with me" (Ex. 33:12). Moses was saying, "God, You're giving me a big job, but You haven't even told me who's going to help."

In verse 13 Moses says, "If I have found grace in thy sight, show me now thy way, that I may know thee." In other words, "God, I believe You're out there, but give me a demonstration that You're going to be with me in this very difficult task." In verse 14 God replies, "My presence shall go with thee." Moses knew what that meant; in verse 18 he says, "I beseech thee, show me Thy glory." The presence of God was His manifest glory.

(*b*) God's response

God said, "I will make all my goodness pass before thee, and I will proclaim the name of the Lord before thee, and will be gracious to whom I will be gracious, and will show mercy on whom I will show mercy" (v. 19). In other words, "You will see My goodness, My name (the embodiment of all My attributes), My grace, and My mercy." The glory of God includes all His attributes. God reduced them to a glorious light so that Moses could see them.

In verses 22-23 God says, "It shall come to pass, while my glory passeth by, that I will put thee in a cleft of the rock, and will cover thee with my hand while I pass by; and I will take away mine hand, and thou shalt see my back; but my face shall not be seen." No one

14

could see the full glory of God and live (v. 20), so God said, "I'm going to let you see a little of My afterglow." Moses saw God's glory, and his face glowed like a light bulb when he came down the mountain. Those who saw him were shocked (Ex. 34:29-30). God was using Moses to say, "People of Israel, will you see My glory?"

(3) The cloud and pillar of fire

When the Israelites moved into the wilderness, they were led by a great white cloud in the daytime and a pillar of fire at night (Ex. 13:21). God was again saying, "See My glory—the fullness of My attributes." But even though they saw His glory every day and night in the wilderness, the Israelites murmured, complained, and disobeyed. They were so faithless that the first generation from Egypt died in the wilderness. Man again turned his back on God's glory.

(4) The Tabernacle

Exodus 40:34 says that when the Tabernacle had been built, "a cloud covered the tent of the congregation, and the glory of the Lord filled the tabernacle." The Tabernacle was a place of worship. The twelve tribes of Israel camped in a circle around it so they could focus on God's glory. The glory would descend when God wanted them to camp, and it would return to the sky when He wanted them to move. But though God's glory dwelt in their midst, the people still griped and disobeyed.

(5) The Temple

(a) The display of God's glory

When Solomon had built the Temple, "it came to pass, when the priests were come out of the holy place, that the cloud filled the house of the Lord, so that the priests could

15

not stand to minister because of the cloud; for the glory of the Lord had filled the house of the Lord" (1 Kings 8:10-11). The Temple was a magnificent edifice, unequaled in the world. From it God was again saying to the people, "See My glory. Focus on it. Recognize who I am, and give Me proper reverence and worship."

(b) The defiling of God's glory

Later in history, the prophet Ezekiel had a vision of the Temple: "He [the Lord] brought me to the door of the court; and when I looked, behold, a hole in the wall. Then said he unto me, Son of man, dig now in the wall; and when I had digged in the wall, behold, a door. And he said unto me, Go in. . . . So I went in and saw; and, behold, every form of creeping things, and abominable beasts, and all the idols of the house of Israel, portrayed upon the wall round about" (Ezek. 8:7-10).

The people had turned the Temple of God into a place of idolatry, fitting the description of the godless in Romans 1:21-23 by worshiping images of "creeping things." In addition, men had usurped the place of priests and worshiped the sun and Tammuz, an ancient fertility god (Ezek. 8:11-16).

(c) The departure of God's glory

Ezekiel 10:18-19 and 11:22-23 tell us that God removed His glory from the Temple in response to the wickedness of the people.

(6) Christ

John 1:14 says, "The Word [God] was made flesh, and dwelt among us (and we beheld his glory, the glory as of the only begotten of the Father)." Jesus was the embodiment of God's glory. On the mount of transfiguration (Luke 9:28-36), Jesus pulled back His flesh, so to speak, and Peter, James, and John "saw His glory." God revealed His glory in Jesus Christ, but the world rejected Him.

b) In the future

When Christ returns, He will come "in the clouds of heaven with power and great glory" (Matt. 24:30). Revelation 6:15-16 says that people will cry for the rocks and mountains to fall on them to hide them from His face. I believe He will come in blazing glory, blinding the world. His glory will fill the whole earth (cf. Num. 14:21), and then all creation will worship Him. Ultimately, God will receive the full glory due Him.

c) In the present

In Ephesians 3:19-21 Paul expresses his desire that we "be filled with all the fullness of God. Now unto him who is able to do exceedingly abundantly above all that we ask or think, . . . unto him be glory in the church." Presently the glory of God is displayed in the church.

Colossians 1:27 says "Christ in you, [is] the hope of glory" and 2 Corinthians 4:6 says that "God, who commanded the light to shine out of darkness, hath shone in our hearts, to give the light of the knowledge of the glory of God in the face of Jesus Christ." If the glory of God in the face of Christ is to be seen by anyone today, it must shine through us. Believers are called to "adorn the doctrine of God" (Titus 2:10), thus manifesting His glory.

4. The rejection of God's glory

Nothing is more important to God than His glory. In Isaiah 48:11 He says, "I will not give my glory unto another." He has created everything to glorify Himself; therefore He strongly opposes those who act contrary to that purpose.

a) Jeremiah 13:15-16—"Hear, and give ear; be not proud; for the Lord hath spoken. Give glory to the Lord, your God, before he cause darkness, and before your feet stumble upon the dark mountains, and, while ye look for light, he turn it into the shadow of death, and make it gross darkness." Pride causes man to seek glory for himself and makes him unable to glorify God, bringing about serious consequences.

Verse 17 says, "But if ye will not hear it, my soul shall weep in secret places for your pride; and mine eye shall weep bitterly, and run down with tears." The prophet's lament shows that it breaks God's heart when people don't glorify Him because they put themselves in the place of judgment.

b) Daniel 4:30—King Nebuchadnezzar said, "Is not this great Babylon, that I have built . . . for the honor of my majesty?" Having accomplished some great things, he was saying, "How wonderful I am! Look what I've done!" Verse 31 says, "While the word was in the king's mouth, there fell a voice from heaven, saying, O King Nebuchadnezzar, to thee it is spoken, The kingdom is departed from thee." He had gone too far—no one can compete with God. Nebuchadnezzar was like King Uzziah, of whom the Bible says, "When he was strong, his heart was lifted up to his destruction" (2 Chron. 26:16). God gave Uzziah leprosy, and he was never healed (2 Chron. 26:19-21).

Nebuchadnezzar's story continues in verses 32-33: "They shall drive thee from men, and thy dwelling shall be with the beasts of the field; they shall make thee to eat grass like oxen, and seven times shall pass over thee, until thou know that the Most High ruleth in the kingdom of men, and giveth it to whomsoever he will. The same hour was the thing fulfilled upon Nebuchadnezzar, and he was driven from men, and did eat grass like oxen, and his body was wet with the dew of heaven, till his hairs were grown like eagles' feathers, and his nails like birds' claws." The mighty king had become a raving maniac in the wilderness.

Verse 34 says, "At the end of the days I, Nebuchadnezzar, lifted up mine eyes unto heaven, and mine understanding returned unto me, and I blessed the Most High, and I praised and honored Him who liveth forever, whose dominion is an everlasting dominion, and His kingdom is from generation to generation." He finally realized that only God deserved glory.

c) Acts 12:21-23—Here we read of God's judgment upon Herod Agrippa I, the king of Palestine from A.D. 41 to 44: "Upon a set day Herod, arrayed in royal apparel, sat upon his throne, and made an oration unto them. And the people gave a shout, saying, It is the voice of a god, and not of a man. And immediately an angel of the Lord smote him, because he gave not God the glory; and he was eaten of worms, and died." An abrupt ending to Herod's big day!

We either glorify God or we pay the price. The generation that failed to see the glory of God on the face of Moses, in the cloud and pillar of fire, and in the Tabernacle was destroyed in the wilderness. The people who refused to see the glory of God in the Temple were also set aside. Similarly, the generation that didn't see the glory of God in Jesus Christ was cut off from the blessing of God. And whoever refuses to recognize the glory of God before Jesus Christ returns in blazing glory will know a Christless, godless eternity. Romans 1:28 says that when men failed to glorify God, He "gave them over to a reprobate mind," a doomed existence.

God wants us to see His glory and judges those who do not glorify Him. Because God's glory is so important to Him, we must focus on it to grow spiritually.

E. The Progression of Spiritual Growth

First John 2:12-14 lists the three basic levels of spiritual growth. John used an analogy of physical human growth. In verse 12 he says, "I write unto you, little children, because your sins are forgiven you for his name's sake." At first, John referred to all believers with one term—"little children," which simply means "offspring." It has nothing to do with age and could refer to someone who is eighty-five years old.

However, in verses 13-14 John uses different terms, dividing the children of God into three categories: "I write unto you, fathers, because ye have known him that is from the beginning. I write unto you, young men, because ye have overcome the wicked one. I write unto you, little children [lit. "babies," a different Greek word than in verse 12], because ye have known the Father. I have written unto you, fathers, because ye have known Him that is from the beginning. I have written unto you, young men, because ye are strong, and the word of God abideth in you, and ye have overcome the wicked one." These are the three levels of spiritual growth: little children, young men, and fathers.

1. "Little children"

   In verse 13 John says, "I write unto you, little children, because ye have known the Father." What is the first thing a child recognizes? His parents. The spiritual child realizes he is a child of God—and not much else.

2. "Young men"

   John then said, "I write unto you, young men, because you have overcome the wicked one." Satan is the wicked one. How do you overcome Satan? Verse 14 says, "Because ye are strong, and the word of God abideth in you, . . . ye have overcome the wicked one."

   Little children do not have the Word of God abiding in them strongly—they know only the basics. Consequently, they can be "tossed to and fro, and carried about with every wind of doctrine" (Eph. 4:14). That's why when you lead someone to Christ, the first thing you need to do is get him grounded in the Word so he doesn't get confused by false doctrine. A spiritual young man is strong in the Word and has overcome the wicked one. Because Satan is a liar (John 8:44) and appears as an angel of light (2 Cor. 11:14), he is the master of false religion. But a spiritual young man understands doctrine and is not victimized by false religion.

A Personal Spiritual Progression

My own experience has taught me about the different levels of spiritual growth. When I was a spiritual babe, I was lost in the euphoria of loving the Lord and didn't know much theology. At that time I was easily influenced by anyone's teaching. But later, when I had learned the Word of God, false doctrine no longer deceived me; it made me angry. I've also discipled people while they were becoming "young men." Often they want to charge out with their new knowledge, fight the cults, and straighten out the world.

3. "Fathers"

John describes an even deeper level of spiritual growth in verse 13: "I write unto you, fathers, because ye have known him that is from the beginning." It's one thing to know you belong to the family of God and to know the Word of God, but it's another to know God intimately. Spiritual fathers not only know the Bible, but they also deeply know the God who wrote it.

Spiritual growth progresses from knowing you are a Christian to knowing the Word of God to knowing God Himself. The way to know God is to spend your life focusing on His glory, thus learning to understand the fullness of His person. That focus becomes a magnet drawing the believer upward through the levels of maturity.

"All things were created by him, and for him," says Colossians 1:16. He made us for Himself that we might know Him in His fullness. Romans 11:36 says that "of him, and through him, and to him, are all things: to whom be glory forever. Amen." As you focus on the glory of God and begin to honor Him, you will find yourself being changed into His very image as you grow from one level of glory to the next. That is spiritual growth. As we progress in our study, you will learn how to unlock your own potential for spiritual growth.

1. What are two scriptures that command us to grow spiritually (see p. 8)?
2. Does a person grow into a Christian? Why or why not (see p. 8)?
3. What negative effect can knowledge have on the believer (see p. 9)?
4. Give an example of people who were busy with religious activities but far from the truth (see p. 10).
5. Give a simple definition of spiritual growth (see p. 10).
6. What is the "master key" to spiritual growth (see p. 10)?
7. What is the chief end of man, according to the Westminster Shorter Catechism (see p. 11)?
8. According to 2 Corinthians 3:18, what happens to believers as they focus on the glory of the Lord (see pp. 11-12)?
9. What is the power behind spiritual growth (see p. 12)?
10. What is mankind's basic problem, according to Romans 1:21? What is the result of that problem (see p. 12)?
11. Why were Adam and Eve cut off from experiencing the presence of God's glory (see p. 13)?
12. How did the people of Israel typically respond to the revelation of God's glory (see pp. 14-16)?
13. When will God ultimately receive the glory He is due (see p. 17)?
14. How is the glory of God displayed to men today (see p. 17)?
15. What happened to Nebuchadnezzar when he failed to give God the glory (Dan. 4:31-33)? What happened to Herod (Acts 12:21-23; see pp. 18-19)?
16. How did the apostle John define a spiritual child? a spiritual young man? a spiritual father (1 John 2:12-14; see pp. 20-21)?

Pondering the Principles

1. Review the section called "Observations About Spiritual Growth" (see pp. 8-10). Have concepts such as time, knowledge, and prosperity been too prominent in your understanding of spiritual growth? How has that understanding changed after this study? Think about how those concepts do relate to spiritual growth. For instance, is God's love a motivation for growth? What kind of activity might help you to grow?

2. Does your life glorify God? Why or why not? The chapters you're about to read describe many practical ways in which believers can bring glory to God. Before reading them, write down your own list. Support your ideas with Scripture.

3. Knowing God intimately is the highest level of spiritual growth (see p. 21). To understand what that means, think of the people you are close to. You deeply desire to be with them, give to them, and introduce them to others. Your love and commitment to them grows over the years as well. Is your relationship with God like that? Think about how you can get to know Him better.

2
Confessing Jesus as Lord and Glorifying God

Outline

Introduction

Lesson
I. Confessing Jesus as Lord
  A. The Reasons for Salvation
    1. The main reason
    2. The lesser reasons
      a) To keep people out of hell
      b) To manifest God's love
      c) To obey Christ's command
  B. The Rejection of Salvation
  C. The Response to Salvation
II. Aiming Our Lives at Glorifying God
  A. By Being Willing to Sacrifice All
    1. Illustrated by Christ
    2. Illustrated by Peter
      a) His privilege
      b) His impatience
      c) His eventual sacrifice
    3. Illustrated by Paul
    4. Illustrated by Christian missionaries
    5. Illustrated by the heroes of faith
    6. Illustrated by Hugh Latimer and Nicholas Ridley
    7. Illustrated by Savonarola
    8. Illustrated by John Paton

B. By Being Sensitive to the Heart of God
   1. Exemplified by David
   2. Exemplified by the church at Ephesus
   3. Exemplified by a new Christian
C. By Being Humble
   1. The attitude of humility
   2. An illustration of humility
      a) Paul's experiences
      b) Paul's influence
      c) Paul's young opponents
      d) Paul's attitude
         (1) He rejoiced in the boldness of his followers
         (2) He rejoiced in the preaching of the gospel
D. By Being Joyful in Trials

Introduction

Bringing glory to God is the master key to spiritual growth. In the remainder of this study we will discuss many practical ways in which we can glorify God.

Lesson

I. CONFESSING JESUS AS LORD

A life that glorifies God must focus initially on the lordship of Christ.

A. The Reasons for Salvation

   1. The main reason

      Philippians 2:5-8 discusses the humiliation (Gk., *kenosis*) of Christ, explaining how He took the form of a man and humbled Himself, even to the point of death on a cross. Verses 9-11 say, "Wherefore, God . . . hath highly exalted him, and given him a name which is above every name, that at the name of Jesus every knee should bow, of things in heaven, and things in earth, and things under the earth, and that every tongue should confess that Jesus Christ is Lord, to the glory of God, the Father."

Because of Jesus' great act of obedience, the Father has exalted Him and called everything in the universe to confess Him as Lord. That brings glory to God.

2. The lesser reasons

Most people probably think we should be saved for reasons other than the glory of God. Christians will usually give the following as the primary reasons they witness:

a) To keep people out of hell

They want people to avoid eternal punishment.

b) To manifest God's love

Some will say, "God loves them and I love them, so I tell them about Christ."

c) To obey Christ's command

Christ commands us to evangelize (Matt. 28:18-20; Acts 1:8).

Those are all valid biblical reasons for evangelism, but the main reason we should preach the gospel is for the glory of God (Phil. 1:11).

B. The Rejection of Salvation

To live without salvation is to deny Christ, which is the greatest affront to God.

1. John 16:9—Jesus said He would send the Holy Spirit to convict the world "of sin, because they believe not on me." The greatest sin anyone can commit is failing to believe in Jesus Christ.

2. John 5:23—"All men should honor the Son, even as they honor the Father. He that honoreth not the Son honoreth not the Father, who hath sent him." You can-

not give glory to God unless you give glory to His Son, who is the fullness of His glory.

C. The Response to Salvation

To give glory to Christ, we must confess Him as Lord. That's part of salvation, not a subsequent act. You can't say, "I've taken Him as Savior, and later on I'll make Him Lord." Those are not two distinct decisions. When you are saved, you confess Christ as Lord. Romans 10:9 says, "If thou shalt confess with thy mouth the Lord Jesus, and shalt believe in thine heart that God hath raised Him from the dead, thou shalt be saved." Salvation is a matter of confessing that Christ is God and therefore sovereign.

Jesus Comes As Is

Someone once asked me if I was a "lordship salvationist." At the time I wasn't sure what he meant—I thought he was referring to someone who stood on a corner playing a trumpet or beating a drum. He told me, however, that a lordship salvationist is someone who believes you must accept Jesus as Lord to be saved. I said I didn't know any other way to accept Christ. He is Lord and we accept Him on His terms, not ours. We can't redefine Jesus as something less than He is and still have Him. I asked him if Jesus is Lord, and he said yes. I said, "Then how do you take Him?"

We must take Him as He is.

Christ rules the lives of Christians, and the main purpose of preaching the gospel is so He may rule in the lives of others for His glory. In Romans 1:5 Paul says we preach "obedience to the faith among all nations, for his name." We preach the gospel primarily for Jesus' sake (cf. 3 John 7); we want Him to be acknowledged as Lord and to receive glory.

One Man's Passion for Christ's Glory

Englishman Henry Martyn served as a missionary in India and Persia in the late eighteenth and early nineteenth centuries. John

Stott, citing Constance E. Padwick's *Henry Martyn, Confessor of the Faith*, tells us Martyn "turned his back on an academic career and entered the ministry. Two years later . . . he sailed for India. 'Let me burn out for God,' he cried in Calcutta, as he lived in an abandoned Hindu temple. And as he watched the people prostrating themselves before their images, he wrote: 'this excited more horror in me than I can well express.'" When he heard a blasphemous comment about Christ, Martyn responded, "I could not endure existence if Jesus was not glorified; it would be hell to me, if He were to be always thus dishonored" (Stott, *Our Guilty Silence* [Chicago: InterVarsity, 1967], pp. 21-22).

If you have never confessed Jesus Christ as Lord, you have no capacity to live for His glory. You cannot say, "I deny Christ. He is not my Savior or Lord," and then expect to glorify God. If you dishonor the Son, you dishonor the Father (John 5:23). So salvation is the necessary beginning for glorifying God and, therefore, for spiritual growth. You cannot grow until you are born.

II. AIMING OUR LIVES AT GLORIFYING GOD

In 1 Corinthians 10:31 Paul says, "Whether, therefore, ye eat, or drink, or whatever ye do, do all to the glory of God." When you confessed Jesus as Lord, that was done to the glory of God. Now whatever else you do—even the most mundane functions of life such as eating and drinking—should be focused on the glory of God. That should be the underlying attitude of your life.

In John 8:49-50 Jesus says, "I honor my Father. . . . I seek not mine own glory." You will grow spiritually when you follow that example by making God's glory the main focus of your life. If we submit our lives to Christ's lordship, we will be characterized by His humble attitude.

A. By Being Willing to Sacrifice All

1. Illustrated by Christ

In John 12:27 Jesus says, "Now is my soul troubled; and what shall I say? Father, save me from this hour. But for this cause came I unto this hour." In anticipation of the cross Jesus was saying, "God, can I ask you to bail Me out? Of course not—this is what I came here for." Then He said, "Father, glorify thy name. Then came there a voice from heaven, saying, I have both glorified it, and will glorify it again" (v. 28). Christ was about to suffer immeasurable anguish in body and spirit, but He was willing to glorify God despite the cost. You will grow spiritually when you do God's will regardless of the consequences.

2. Illustrated by Peter

John 21 contains another illustration of God's being glorified through sacrifice.

a) His privilege

Peter had been chosen by God before the foundation of the world for some important tasks. He was to be a key leader in the early church as it spread from Jerusalem to the rest of the world. Unfortunately, Peter was inconsistent and uncommitted in his early days of discipleship. He often gave strong verbal assent but failed every time he was tested.

God had shown Peter great things, such as Jesus' walking on water (Matt. 14:22-33), the feeding of five thousand people (14:15-21), and the transfiguration (17:1-13). God's power had enabled Peter to make this great confession of Christ: "Thou art the Christ, the Son of the living God" (16:16). Peter saw soldiers fall backward like dominoes in the Garden of Gethsemane when Jesus spoke (John 18:3-6). Peter had seen the resurrected Christ in the upper room (20:19-23) and even had a personal audience with Him (Luke 24:34). Yet in spite of all that, he remained inconsistent. He probably felt inadequate because of his many failures.

b) His impatience

Following His resurrection, Jesus promised to appear to the disciples in Galilee (Mark 16:7). When Christ didn't arrive immediately, Peter got impatient and said, "I go fishing." (John 21:3). In other words, "I'm going back to what I used to do. I wasn't cut out for the ministry—I've failed every time I've had an opportunity. The one thing I can do is fish, and I'm going back to it." Peter was the leader, so several other disciples followed him.

Verse 3 continues, "They went forth, and entered into a boat." The Greek text is literally translated "the boat," perhaps indicating that they were using Peter's own boat. He was going back to his old profession, and the rest were going with him. But they couldn't catch any fish because the Lord had rerouted every fish in the Sea of Galilee to get His point across. Verse 3 concludes by saying they fished all night and caught nothing.

c) His eventual sacrifice

The Lord appeared in the morning and confronted Peter. After Peter affirmed three times that he loved Him (vv. 15-17), Jesus said, "Verily, verily, I say unto thee, When thou wast young, thou girdedst thyself, and walkedst where thou wouldest" (v. 18). He was saying, "Peter, you've had your own way—putting on your own belt, and going where you wanted." ("Girding oneself" described preparing for a journey.) Then Jesus said, "But when thou shalt be old, thou shalt stretch forth thy hands [a phrase used in extrabiblical literature to speak of crucifixion], and another shall gird thee, and carry thee where thou wouldest not. This spoke he, signifying by what death he should glorify God" (vv. 18-19).

Peter's death would bring glory to God because Peter would be willing to pay any price for his faith. That prophecy must have been a surprise to Peter, who had previously denied Christ under persecution (Mark 14:70-71). But the Lord said to him, "One day you will glorify Me because you will be content to die for My sake."

3. Illustrated by Paul

In Philippians 1:21 Paul says, "To me to live is Christ, and to die is gain." In Romans 14:8 he says, "Whether we live, we live unto the Lord; and whether we die, we die unto the Lord; whether we live, therefore, or die, we are the Lord's" (Rom. 14:8). Every Christian should be willing to glorify God at all costs—even death.

4. Illustrated by Christian missionaries

Missionaries throughout history have been willing to die for Christ.

5. Illustrated by the heroes of faith

No price was too high for the Old Testament heroes of faith in Hebrews 11, "of whom the world was not worthy" (v. 38). Many of them died for their faith.

6. Illustrated by Hugh Latimer and Nicholas Ridley

These two sixteenth-century English reformers sang praises to Christ as they were burned at the stake for their faith.

7. Illustrated by Savonarola

Savonarola, the great fifteenth-century preacher in Italy, was burned at the stake by the system of Rome.

8. Illustrated by John Paton

In the last century, John Paton and his wife were sent from Scotland to the New Hebrides, a group of islands in the western Pacific where only cannibals lived. When they landed, they didn't speak the language, and all they knew about the place was that people had gone there and had never returned. Their lives were constantly threatened. Later, when the chief of the tribe in that area became a Christian, he asked Paton what army protected his place of dwelling when he first arrived. Perhaps God's holy angels became manifest to protect the missionaries.

Paton's wife gave birth not long after they arrived. Both she and the baby died several days later, and Paton slept on their graves for three or four nights to keep the natives from digging up their bodies and eating them. Despite such trials, he devoted the rest of his life to ministering in the New Hebrides. Near the end of his life, Paton said in his autobiography (*The Story of John G. Paton* [New York: A. L. Burt Co., n. d.], compiled by his brother James) that he didn't know of one native who hadn't made at least a profession of faith in Jesus Christ. God used John Paton because he was content to do God's will at any cost.

You can't grow spiritually by charting your own course, saying, "Lord, here's what I will do, and here's what I won't do." You must be willing to be embarrassed, defamed, and dishonored by the world, and settle for fewer possessions in this life. Spiritual growth occurs when you are consumed with God's glory and not your own comfort and plans.

B. By Being Sensitive to the Heart of God

We should be so consumed with God's glory that we hurt when He is dishonored.

1. Exemplified by David

In Psalm 69:9 David says, "The zeal of thine house hath eaten me up; and the reproaches of those who reproached thee are fallen upon me." David was deeply hurt when God was dishonored.

As a father, I understand what David was saying. If you hurt someone in my family, you hurt me. Often I have cried for someone I love whose heart was broken. When you identify with God in that way, you will care about His honor much more than about what happens to you.

2. Exemplified by the church at Ephesus

God commended the church at Ephesus, saying, "Thou canst not bear them who are evil" (Rev. 2:2). They couldn't tolerate evil because it impinged upon God's holiness. Many Christians today, however, are so consumed with their own concerns that they don't feel any pain when God is dishonored.

3. Exemplified by a new Christian

I remember one young girl who learned to feel pain when God was dishonored. She left a little town in West Virginia to live with a guy who was a student at UCLA. After a while, he kicked her out. She wandered around and eventually tried to take her life several times by slashing her wrists, but each time she survived. My sister and I met her and had the opportunity to lead her to Christ. Soon after that she decided to go back to her hometown so she could tell her mother and friends about Christ. The town apparently had no good church, however. I was concerned that there would be no one to disciple her.

Several months later, she wrote me a letter. I was fearful that she had wandered away from God and was writing for counsel in the midst of some terrible situation. But this is what she wrote:

"I hope everything is well with you. I have really begun to put things together in the Bible. By reading the Old Testament I have been able to see that God deserves much more recognition than He's getting. I can see how He gave people so many chances and how they continued to break His heart by worshiping idols and sinning. God wanted the Israelites to sacrifice lambs, goats, oxen and things like that as an atonement to Him for sin. He is God, after all, and He had to have some payment for the trouble and the sins of men.

"To think that God actually talked and was in the visible presence of these people and yet they kept on complaining and sinning! I can almost feel the unbearable sadness that God feels when someone rejects and doesn't glorify Him. He's God! He made us. He gave us everything. We continue to doubt and reject Him. It's awful! When I think of how I hurt Him, I hope I can someday make it up.

"I have a soft spot in my heart for God. I can feel His jealousy now when I see people worshiping idols and other gods. It's all so clear to me that God must be glorified. He deserves it, and it's long overdue. I can't wait to just tell Jesus, and thus God indirectly, that I love Him and just kiss the ground He walks on because He should be worshiped. I want God to be God and to take His rightful place. I'm tired of the way people put Him down."

Obedience to the lordship of Christ includes being able to feel the pain that God feels.

C. By Being Humble

1. The attitude of humility

The person who is truly living for the glory of God will be content to be outdone by others. Jealousy can be a problem in serving God; we are often not as concerned with God's being glorified as we are with who gets the credit. We should rejoice when God's work is accomplished—even when someone does it better than we do.

Solo Night and a Sore Loser

It has been said that when Satan fell, he landed in the choir loft. Sometimes all the members of church choirs want to sing solos and complain when they don't get the chance. They're more concerned with being heard than they are with glorifying God. I know of one pastor who has so many people wanting to sing solos that he has a Solo Night once a year. Each singer is allowed one verse, and they parade across the platform for their big moment.

I also remember two pastors who held a contest to see who could get the most people into Sunday school. The one who lost got sick because he couldn't stand losing to another pastor!

2. An illustration of humility

Philippians 1:14-18 is a wonderful illustration of humility from the life of the apostle Paul.

a) Paul's experiences

Paul was approaching the end of his ministry when he wrote Philippians, but he had been involved in some great adventures through the years. While leading the expansion of the church in Asia Minor and Greece, he preached on Mars' Hill in Athens and accomplished great things in Corinth, Thessalonica, and Berea. He lived through a shipwreck while being transported as a prisoner to Rome, as well as many other experiences.

b) Paul's influence

Because of his missionary tours, Paul was the spiritual father, grandfather, or uncle of nearly every Gentile believer. No man had a greater influence on the early churches than Paul. In fact, he sometimes preached all night when he visited them. On one such occasion, a man fell out of a window during Paul's sermon and died. But Paul raised him from the dead and continued to preach (Acts 20:7-12). Paul was so loved that whenever he came to town everyone embraced him. When he left Miletus, the Ephesian elders "wept much, and fell on Paul's neck, and kissed him, sorrowing" (Acts 20:37-38).

c) Paul's young opponents

By the time he wrote Philippians, however, Paul was in prison and no longer active in worldwide ministry. A new breed of young preachers was capturing the people's attention. They probably learned the best of Paul's material and added new techniques. Because of them, the people may have been forgetting the imprisoned apostle.

The Old, Forgotten Preacher

I remember meeting a dear old man of God in the Midwest some years ago. He had preached for about sixty years, from the age of twenty until he was eighty-one. When I met him, he was ninety-six years old. He sat in the congregation while I preached, paging through a worn-out Bible. No one knew who he was, and I wondered if he was thinking back on the days when he was a shining sword of usefulness for the Lord.

The young preachers criticized Paul, using his imprisonment as an opportunity to gain prominence (Phil. 1:15-16). They probably said, "God is finished with Paul because he's not contemporary," or, "Paul made a big mistake and God had to shelve him."

d) Paul's attitude

Despite opposition, Paul's attitude in prison was one of joyful contentment.

(1) He rejoiced in the boldness of his followers

In Philippians 1:14 Paul says, "Many of the brethren in the Lord, becoming confident by my bonds, are much more bold to speak the word without fear." Some believers had become bolder in their witness because of Paul's example of suffering for Christ.

(2) He rejoiced in the preaching of the gospel

In verses 15-16 Paul says, "Some, indeed, preach Christ even of envy and strife . . . of contention, not sincerely, supposing to add affliction to my bonds." Paul's opponents were jealous of his achievements and tried to make his imprisonment worse through criticism.

But Paul did not complain. Rather he said, "What then? Notwithstanding, every way, whether in pretense or in truth, Christ is preached; and in that I do rejoice, yea, and will rejoice" (v. 18). He was saying, "As long as Christ is preached, who cares what they say about me?" Only a mature, humble man could say that.

D. By Being Joyful in Trials

In his first epistle, Peter was writing to a group of believers who were suffering because of their obedience to Christ. First Peter 4:14 says, "If ye be reproached for the name of Christ, happy are ye; for the Spirit of glory and of God resteth upon you." Our natural tendency is to become angry and retaliate under persecution, but Peter said we should be happy. Being reproached is a special blessing because it indicates that we have the Spirit. The verse concludes, "On their part, [Christ] is evil spoken of, but on your part he is glorified." Our attitude in trials should be one of joy because God is being glorified. Perhaps the best illustration of that is the cross, where Jesus glorified God through the worst suffering imaginable.

Verses 15-16 continue, "Let none of you suffer as a murderer, or as a thief, or as an evildoer, or as a busybody in other men's matters. Yet, if any man suffer as a Christian, let him not be ashamed, but let him glorify God on this behalf." We should be glad to suffer for Christ.

One of the characteristics of life is growth. If you don't want to grow spiritually, that may indicate you are not a Christian. If you do want to grow, you must obey Jesus Christ by being willing to pay any price, hurt when He is dishonored, and have a humble attitude toward others. Then you will be able to rejoice when suffering for Him.

Confronting an Evil World

No one can live for God's glory and be entirely comfortable in this world. You shouldn't be obnoxious or try to be a misfit, but if your life is Christlike, you will bear some of the reproach He bore. We live in a day when many want to make Christianity easy, but the Bible makes it hard. Many want to make Christians lovable, but God says they'll be reproachable. Christianity must confront the system by being distinct from it. It must expose sin before it can disclose the remedy.

Focusing on the Facts

1. Give some reasons that people witness. What should be the main reason (see pp. 26-27)?
2. What is the greatest affront to God (see p. 27)?
3. Name a verse that says we must confess Jesus as Lord for salvation (see p. 28).
4. What principle of glorifying God does Jesus Christ illustrate in John 12:27-28 (see pp. 29-30)?
5. Give some examples from church history of people who paid a great price for the sake of God's glory (see pp. 32-33).
6. What should be the response of the Christian when God is dishonored? Give some examples of that response (see pp. 33-34).
7. What should be our attitude when someone else does God's work better than we do (see p. 35)?
8. What principle of glorifying God does Paul illustrate in Philippians 1:14-18? How (see pp. 35-36)?
9. Why is there blessing in being reproached for Christ's sake (1 Pet. 4:14-16; see p. 38)?
10. What is the best illustration of God's being glorified through suffering (see p. 38)?

Pondering the Principles

1. Any efforts at spiritual growth are futile without salvation because one cannot grow until he is born. Do you know for sure that you are a child of God? Second Corinthians 13:5 says, "Examine yourselves, whether you are in the faith; prove yourselves." To do that, read 1 John, which was written "that you may know that you have eternal life" (5:13, NASB*).

2. Ask yourself some practical questions about three of the principles discussed in this chapter. Sacrifice: What price are you willing to pay for God to be glorified? Are you willing to suffer and die for Him if necessary? Sensitivity: Does it hurt you when God is dishonored? Have you shed more tears over His pain than over yours? Humility: Would you be willing to serve God in a way that earned you no recognition whatsoever? Do you rejoice when someone outdoes you in God's work?

*New American Standard Bible.

39

3. Have you ever been persecuted for your faith in Christ? If so, can you say it made you happy? In addition to the fact that it glorifies God (see p. 38), consider these other scriptural truths about suffering for Christ: it is inevitable because it is part of our calling (Phil. 1:29, 1 Thess. 3:3-4; 2 Tim. 3:12; 1 Pet. 2:20-21), the persecuted will be rewarded and the persecutor punished (Matt. 5:10-12; Rom. 8:18; 2 Thess. 1:4-10), and persecution is a proof of true faith (Matt. 10:22; Phil. 1:28; 2 Thess. 1:4-5).

3
Confessing Our Sins

Outline

Introduction and Review
  A. The Progression of Spiritual Growth
  B. The Master Key to Spiritual Growth
 I. Confessing Jesus as Lord
II. Aiming Our Lives at Glorifying God
  A. By Being Willing to Sacrifice All
  B. By Being Sensitive to the Heart of God
  C. By Being Humble
  D. By Being Joyful in Trials

Lesson
III. Confessing Our Sins
  A. Confession Demonstrated
     1. Achan
        a) The confrontation
        b) The confession
        c) The chastening
     2. The thief on the cross
     3. The Philistines
        a) Their conflict with Israel
           (1) The folly of the Israelites
           (2) The fear of the Philistines
           (3) The flight of the Israelites
        b) Their problems with the Ark
           (1) In Ashdod
           (2) In Gath
           (3) In Ekron
        c) Their confession of sin

B. Confession Described
   1. Taking responsibility
   2. Taking sin seriously
   3. Agreeing with God
   4. Repenting of our sin
   5. Examining our lives
      a) In response to chastening
      b) In response to guilt

Introduction and Review

All Christians are in the process of spiritual growth regardless of how long they have been saved. That growth will not stop until we achieve instant perfection in the presence of the Lord, so the truths we are learning in these studies are important for everyone.

A. The Progression of Spiritual Growth

As we have seen, 1 John 2:13-14 discusses three stages of spiritual growth: babies, young men, and fathers (see pp. 19-21). The spiritual father is one who truly knows God. Spiritual growth, therefore, is an ascension toward that goal of knowing God. The apostle Paul continued in the process of spiritual growth even after he had reached a high level. At the height of his life and ministry—when he had accomplished most of his dreams and desires—his goal was still "that I may know him" (Phil. 3:10). Despite his maturity, Paul longed for an increasingly deep, vital, and fulfilling comprehension of the God he loved and served.

Old vs. New

When we are first saved, our new spiritual nature and the sinful flesh perform a sort of balancing act. Though we struggle against it, sin may often be strong enough to offset our attempts at holiness. But as we mature, there will be a decreased frequency of sinfulness and a proportional increase in righteousness. We never become totally sinless in this life, however—the process continues throughout our lives. Paul said, "Not as though I had already attained. . . . I press toward the mark" (Phil. 3:12, 14). The evidence of growth is a decrease in sin.

I have seen that struggle in my own life. When I was first saved, I felt much like Paul in Romans 7. What I wanted to do, I didn't do; and what I didn't want to do, I did. Yet as I have grown, the power and frequency of sin in my life has decreased.

B. The Master Key to Spiritual Growth

Glorifying God is the master key to spiritual growth. Therefore, Christians grow only when they are living for God's glory.

Second Corinthians 3:18 says, "We all, with unveiled face beholding as in a mirror the glory of the Lord, are changed into the same image from glory to glory, even as by the Spirit of the Lord." As we focus on God's glory in the Word, we grow spiritually through the work of the Holy Spirit. Any time we live merely for ourselves, our growth stops.

In this study we are searching the Scriptures for some practical ways to glorify God with our lives.

I. CONFESSING JESUS AS LORD (see pp. 25-29)

II. AIMING OUR LIVES AT GLORIFYING GOD (see pp. 29-38)

A. By Being Willing to Sacrifice All (see pp. 29-33)

B. By Being Sensitive to the Heart of God (see pp. 33-35)

C. By Being Humble (see pp. 35-37)

D. By Being Joyful in Trials (see p. 38)

The Success Syndrome

American society is breeding a generation of Christians who primarily want to be successful. Seldom do they have a humble attitude of service that says, "I will give my life for the glory of God no matter what it costs me." To draw a big crowd of Christians today, the church often gets a celebrity—Miss America, a wealthy businessman, the president of a company, a Hollywood personality, a famous athlete, or a politician. That has created a model of personal success rather than of service.

Today many who consider themselves to be Christians are often unwilling to make sacrifices or die for the cause of Christ because they have been taught, whether verbally or not, that Christians should be rich, famous, successful, and popular. That orientation toward personal success rather than humble service is the opposite of what glorifies God. Living for the glory of God means knowing you're expendable and being ready to die, if necessary, to accomplish God's ends. As Paul said, "If I be offered upon the sacrifice and service of your faith, I joy, and rejoice with you all" (Phil. 2:17). Such a humble attitude glorifies God.

Unfortunately, many people want to serve the Lord only if it's on their conditions in the perfect environment. They want all the success factors built in. Where are the humble people willing to risk obscurity for the great adventure of glorifying God?

To grow spiritually, we must lose ourselves in the lordship of Christ at the moment of salvation and allow Him to dominate our lives from then on. In doing so, we must seek only His glory—not our own comfort or success. We will not grow when we choose our own way or serve God with the wrong motive.

Lesson

III. CONFESSING OUR SINS

Confessing our sins is an expression of humility (see pp. 35-37) and a major key to spiritual growth, but it is difficult to do. We are all prone to shift the responsibility for sin away from ourselves and blame our circumstances, our environment, or other people. In doing so we fail to glorify God.

A. Confession Demonstrated

1. Achan

Joshua 7 shows how confession glorifies God. Moses had forfeited his right to enter the Promised Land by disobeying God at the rock (cf. Num. 20:7-13), so Joshua led the children of Israel to their first great victory at Jericho (Josh. 6:1-21). Beforehand, he cautioned them not to take any spoils from the city (v. 18). He didn't want them to have any remnants of a pagan society. However, a man named Achan took spoils from the city, and as a result Israel was defeated in their next battle, at Ai (Josh. 7:1-5).

a) The confrontation

When Joshua found out about Achan's sin, he said to him, "My son, give, I pray thee, glory to the Lord God of Israel, and make confession unto Him, and tell me now what thou hast done; hide it not from me" (Josh. 7:19). Joshua told Achan to glorify God by confessing his sin.

b) The confession

"Achan answered Joshua, and said, Indeed, I have sinned against the Lord God of Israel, and thus and thus have I done" (v. 20).

c) The chastening

Verse 24-25 tell us that "Joshua, and all the children of Israel with him, took Achan, the son of Zerah, and the silver, and the garment, and the wedge of gold [all that he had taken], and his sons, and his daughters, and his oxen, and his asses, and his sheep, and his tent, and all that he had; and they brought them unto the valley of Achor. And Joshua said, Why hast thou troubled us? The Lord shall trouble thee this day. And all Israel stoned him." Notice that Achan was punished even though he confessed his sin.

Confession doesn't preclude chastening. David also confessed his sin in Psalms 32 and 51, but that didn't eliminate the consequences.

After the Israelites stoned Achan and his family, they "burned them with fire. . . . And they raised over [them] a great heap of stones unto this day. So the Lord turned from the fierceness of his anger. Wherefore the name of that place was called, The valley of Achor, unto this day" (vv. 25-26). Achor means "trouble" in Hebrew. God was saying to Israel, "If you disobey Me, there will be severe consequences." Achan and his family (evidently also implicated in the crime) were all put to death.

Why did Joshua want Achan to confess his sin? Because God would have looked like a cruel ogre if He had taken the life of that man and his family without anyone's knowing why. When Achan confessed his sin, he was saying, "God, You have every right to punish me because I deserve it." That is why confession brings glory to God. When God chastens us for our sin—which He must do because He is holy—He will look unfair in the eyes of others unless we admit we deserve it. Achan said, "I have sinned against the Lord God of Israel." He didn't blame God, the circumstances, or others but accepted the responsibility for his sin.

2. The thief on the cross

The thief who hung on a cross beside Jesus Christ had dishonored God all his life. But in his last moments, he gave glory to God. In Luke 23:41 he said to the other thief, "We, indeed, [suffer] justly," which was to say, "What are you complaining about? We are getting exactly what we deserve." The thief realized that God was righteous in His judgment.

Excuses, Excuses

Whenever we excuse our sin, we are blaming God. Adam did that when God questioned him about eating the forbidden fruit. He answered, "The woman whom thou gavest to be with me, she gave me of the tree" (Gen. 3:12). Adam did not accept responsibility for his sin but blamed God, who had given Eve to him.

Sin is never God's fault, nor is it the fault of a person or circumstance that God brings into our lives. Excusing sin impugns God for something that is our fault alone. If He chooses to chasten us, it is because we deserve it.

Tossing Aside the Dead Weight

Confession of sin is essential to spiritual growth. When you openly face the reality of your sin and confess it, you then have less dead weight to drag you down in the process of growth. Hebrews 12:1 says, "Let us lay aside every weight, and the sin which doth so easily beset us, and let us run with patience the race that is set before us." Our growth increases as the weight of sin drops off through confession.

3. The Philistines

We find another illustration of confession in 1 Samuel.

a) Their conflict with Israel

(1) The folly of the Israelites

The children of Israel had ignored God for a long time. Instead, they had been pursuing their own ends. They were still religious in a formal and ritualistic sense, but their hearts were empty toward God. In 1 Samuel 4 they were about to engage in a battle with the Philistines, whom they knew could overpower them militarily. In their fear they decided they needed God if they were going to defend themselves. So they got the Ark of the Covenant, in which God's presence resided, and brought it into their camp.

47

(2) The fear of the Philistines

When the Israelites returned with the Ark, "the Philistines were afraid; for they said, God is come into the camp" (v. 7). To the Philistines, the Ark was a god similar to their idols—but more powerful. They said, "Woe unto us! . . . These are the gods that smote the Egyptians with all the plagues in the wilderness" (v. 8).

(3) The flight of the Israelites

The Philistines had to fight, however, and the results were surprising. "Israel was smitten, and they fled every man into his tent: and there was a very great slaughter; for there fell of Israel thirty thousand footmen. And the ark of God was taken; and the two sons of Eli [the high priest], Hophni and Phinehas, were slain" (vv. 10-11). Israel had expected to win because they had the Ark, but instead they were crushed. God would not allow them to view Him as a utilitarian genie whom they could use when they wanted something done and ignore the rest of the time.

b) Their problems with the Ark

The Philistines also experienced the judgment of God.

(1) In Ashdod

First Samuel 5:1-2 says, "The Philistines took the ark of God, and brought it from Ebenezer unto Ashdod. . . . They brought it into the house of Dagon, and set it by Dagon." Dagon was the Philistine god—half fish and half man. "When they of Ashdod arose early on the next day, behold, Dagon was fallen upon his face to the earth before the ark of the Lord. And they took Dagon, and set him in his place again. And when they arose early on the next morning, behold, Dagon was fallen upon his face to the ground before the ark of the Lord; and the head of Dagon and both the palms of his hands were cut off upon the threshold; only the stump of Dagon was left to him" (vv. 3-4). God was saying, "Don't pick him up again; he's right where he belongs!" He will not tolerate any gods or idols being compared to Him.

Verse 6 says, "The hand of the Lord was heavy upon them of Ashdod, and he destroyed them, and smote them with tumors, even Ashdod and its borders." Many of the people died in a plague that was brought on by mice (vv. 4-5), and those who didn't die from the plague were afflicted with tumors.

(2) In Gath

The men of Ashdod realized that the Ark of God was causing their trouble, so they sent it to Gath (the town Goliath came from). That was no great favor to the people of Gath—they were soon plagued with mice and tumors as well. First Samuel 5:9 says, "The hand of the Lord was against the city with a very great destruction; and he smote the men of the city, both small and great, and they had tumors in their secret parts."

(3) In Ekron

The Gathites wanted to get rid of the Ark, so they sent it to Ekron. Once again, "there was a deadly destruction throughout all the city. . . . And the men that died not [from the plague] were smitten with the tumors; and the cry of the city went up to heaven" (vv. 11-12).

c) Their confession of sin

First Samuel 6:1-3 says, "The ark of the Lord was in the country of the Philistines seven months. And the Philistines called for the priests and the diviners, saying, What shall we do to the ark of the Lord? Tell us in what way we shall send it to its place. And they said, If ye send away the ark of the God of Israel, send it not empty; but by all means return him a trespass offering; then ye shall be healed." A trespass offering acknowledges sin. The Philistines realized they had dishonored God and therefore deserved His judgment. They showed they were willing to take the blame by giving Him a trespass offering.

Pagan Votive Offerings

First Samuel 6:4 says, "Then said they, What shall be the trespass offering which we shall return to him? They answered, Five golden tumors, and five golden mice." The Philistines were unfamiliar with Levitical trespass offerings, so they sent a pagan votive offering. One type of votive offering was a symbolic replica of the problem supposedly caused by offending a god. For example, if a pagan had a withered hand, he might assume that the gods had given it to him because he had dishonored them. So he would fashion a clay hand and place it in the temple, acknowledging his sin against the gods.

When I visited the city of Corinth, I went into a little room in a museum where they kept votive offerings that had been recovered. I saw clay replicas of nearly every organ and limb of the body. When people came to worship the god Asclepius (the god of healing), they brought those symbols, acknowledging that their disease was a result of their failure to fulfill the will of the gods.

The Philistines knew that the mice and tumors were a result of God's judgment on them. So their religious officials said, "Ye shall make images of your tumors, and images of your mice that mar the land; and ye shall give glory unto the God of Israel" (v. 5). They glorified God by confessing their sin and acknowledging that He had the right to punish them.

B. Confession Described

1. Taking responsibility

As long as you are making excuses for your sin, you will never grow spiritually. For your life to have a decreasing frequency of sin, which is necessary for growth, you must acknowledge your responsibility. Don't blame your circumstances, your husband, your wife, your boyfriend, your girlfriend, your boss, your employees, or your pastor. Don't even blame the devil. Your sin is your fault. Certainly anything in the world's system contributes to the problem, but sin ultimately occurs as an act of the will—and you are responsible for it.

a) Nehemiah 9:33—Nehemiah said to God, "Thou art just in all that is brought upon us."

b) Luke 15:21—When the prodigal son returned home to his loving father, he said, "I have sinned against heaven, and in thy sight." He was even willing to be treated as a humble laborer because he knew he didn't deserve anything (v. 19). That is the attitude of a person who confesses his sin.

c) Psalm 51:4—David said, "Against thee, thee only, have I sinned, and done this evil in thy sight." David didn't blame anyone but himself.

Confession is acknowledging that your sin is your fault.

2. Taking sin seriously

Confession acknowledges that wrong actions are sin, which is an affront to God's holy nature.

a) Genesis 41:9—"Then spoke the chief butler unto Pharaoh, saying, I do remember my faults this day."

b) Genesis 44:16—"Judah said, What shall we say unto my lord? What shall we speak? Or how shall we clear ourselves? God hath found out the iniquity of thy servants."

c) 1 Samuel 15:24—"Saul said unto Samuel, I have sinned; for I have transgressed the commandment of the Lord."

d) 2 Samuel 12:13—"David said unto Nathan, I have sinned against the Lord."

e) Daniel 9:20—Daniel said, "I was speaking, and praying, and confessing my sin."

f) Luke 5:8—"Simon Peter . . . fell down at Jesus' knees, saying, Depart from me; for I am a sinful man, O Lord."

g) Luke 18:13—"The tax collector, standing afar off, would not lift up so much as his eyes unto heaven, but smote upon his breast, saying, God be merciful to me a sinner."

Confession involves recognizing that sin is your fault and that it *is* sin. That understanding is basic to spiritual growth because you are dealing with something that can retard the process.

3. Agreeing with God

The Greek word translated "confess" is *homologeō*. *Logeō* means "to speak" and *homo* means "the same," as in *homogeneous*. So *homologeō* means "to speak the same." Confessing your sin is not begging for forgiveness; rather, it is saying the same thing about your sin that God says.

Saying, "God, please forgive me," is not confessing your sin. God forgave all your sin when you became a Christian. First John 2:12 says, "Your sins are forgiven you for His name's sake." Jesus has already paid the penalty for all your sin, and it doesn't have to be paid again. Ephesians 4:32 says, "Be ye kind one to another, tenderhearted, forgiving one another, even as God, for Christ's sake, hath forgiven you." You are already forgiven; confession is agreeing with God that you are at fault.

A Mark of the Christian

First John 1:9 says, "If we confess our sins, he is faithful and just to forgive us our sins." First John was written to define the difference between a Christian and a non-Christian, and that verse says confession characterizes the former. Verse 10 says, "If we say that we have not sinned, we make him a liar." Unregenerate men deny their sin, but Christians confess it. A true believer recognizes sin and accepts responsibility for it.

Confession of sin doesn't take place only at salvation. It continues, as faith does, throughout the life of the believer. A willingness to confess sin is part of the pattern of life that characterizes every believer. That pattern also includes love (1 John 3:14), obedience (2:3), separation from the world (2:15), and instruction by the Holy Spirit (2:27). Of course there are varying degrees of confession—sometimes we don't make as full a confession as we should—but a true believer sooner or later acknowledges his sin.

4. Repenting of our sin

Many times we don't confess our sin because we're not ready to let go of it. There is no such thing as true confession without repentance. I can remember saying, "Lord, I'm so sorry for doing such and such. I thank You for already forgiving me"—but that was all I said. I reached a milestone in my spiritual life when I began to say, "Lord, thank You for forgiving those sins. I know they did not please You, and I never want to do them again." That's hard to say sometimes because we want to commit certain sins again. We betray a lack of spiritual maturity when we want to eliminate the penalty of sin but retain the pleasure. For confession to be genuine, we must turn from our sins.

5. Examining our lives

Psalm 66:18 says, "If I regard iniquity in my heart, the Lord will not hear me." We can't even commune with God if we are harboring sin, let alone grow spiritually. So there must be confession of sin in our lives.

a) In response to chastening

We must be willing to accept God's chastening. If we feel He is being too rough with us, we should examine our lives to see if we deserve it. Just as parents must provide consequences for a child's misbehavior, God chastens us so that we don't repeat our mistakes.

b) In response to guilt

God has placed a system of guilt in us for our own good. Spiritual life without guilt would be like physical life without pain. Guilt is a defense mechanism; it is like a bell or buzzer that goes off when we sin to lead us to confession. We can relieve that pain in the soul by confronting our sin and saying, "God, I know this is sin against You, and it is my fault. I don't want to do it again. Please give me the strength to walk another path." That admission must be part of our lives before we can grow spiritually, for it eliminates the sin that holds us back.

Focusing on the Facts

1. Why is confessing our sin a difficult thing to do (see p. 44)?
2. Why did Joshua want Achan to confess his sin (see p. 46)?
3. Whom did Adam blame for his sin (see pp. 45-47)?
4. Spiritual growth is likened to a race in Hebrews 12:1. How does that verse describe sin (see p. 47)?
5. Why did God allow Israel to be defeated by the Philistines (see p. 48)?
6. What happened to the Philistine god Dagon when the Ark of the Covenant was placed next to it (1 Sam. 5:3-4; see pp. 48-49)?
7. What happened to the people of Ashdod, Gath, and Ekron because of the Ark (1 Sam. 5:4-12; see pp. 48-49)?
8. What did the Philistines realize they had to do to have peace (1 Sam. 6:1-3; see pp. 49-50)?
9. Describe the votive offering of the Philistines (1 Sam. 6:4; see p. 50).
10. Who is responsible for sin? Support your answer with Scripture (see pp. 50-51).
11. Explain the meaning of the Greek word translated "confess" (see p. 52).
12. What must we do for our confession to be genuine (see p. 53)?
13. Why does God chasten us (see p. 53)?

Pondering the Principles

1. Confession is much more than verbal admission; it is having God's attitude toward sin. Do you hate sin, especially in your own life, as He does (cf. Prov. 6:16-19; Zech. 8:17)? Consider these truths about God's attitude toward sin, and compare them with your own: *God cannot even look upon sin* (Hab. 1:13). Do you avoid exposing yourself to the sin presented in the media, or do you find it interesting? *God confronts men about their sin* (Acts 17:30; cf. John 4:16-18). Do you practice Matthew 18:15-17 when your brother sins, or do you tend to think it's not your business? *God comes alongside men and women in their struggle with sin* (Rom. 8:26; 1 Cor. 10:13). Are you willing to pour your life into a struggling believer?

2. Sometimes we must uncover sin before we can confess it. David prayed, "Search me, O God . . . and see if there be any wicked way in me" (Ps. 139:23-24). As an exercise in confession, read through any New Testament epistle, and write down every command in the text, leaving space in between each as you write. Then, after praying as David did, write down under each command any specific actions or attitudes of yours that fall short. Speak honestly with God about each sin, and resolve not to repeat them. Make this a regular practice in your devotional life, using other epistles and the commands of Jesus.

4
Trust, Praise, and Bearing Fruit

Outline

Review
I. Confessing Jesus as Lord
II. Aiming Our Lives at Glorifying God
III. Confessing Our Sins

Lesson
IV. Trusting God
  A. Examples of Faith
    1. Abraham
      a) The birth of Isaac
      b) The offering of Isaac
    2. Shadrach, Meshach, and Abednego
      a) The test of faith
      b) The testimony of faith
      c) The triumph of faith
    3. Noah
  B. Growing by Faith
V. Bearing Fruit
  A. The Importance of Bearing Fruit
  B. Types of Spiritual Fruit
    1. Action fruit
      a) Leading others to Christ
      b) Giving
      c) Expressing thanks to God
    2. Attitude fruit
VI. Praising God
  A. The Example of the Psalms
  B. The Aspects of Praise

1. Reciting God's attributes
    a) Illustrated in the Old Testament
    b) Applied to our lives today
2. Reciting God's works
    a) As practiced in the psalms
    b) As practiced by Habakkuk
    c) As practiced today
3. Giving thanks for God's attributes and works
    a) Illustrated by a leper
    b) Illustrated by Paul

Review

I. CONFESSING JESUS AS LORD (see pp. 25-29)

II. AIMING OUR LIVES AT GLORIFYING GOD (see pp. 29-38)

III. CONFESSING OUR SINS (see pp. 44-54)

Lesson

IV. TRUSTING GOD

Contrary to the impression given by much of organized religion, with its massive cathedrals and stained-glass windows, glorifying God is as simple as trusting Him.

A. Examples of Faith

1. Abraham

    a) The birth of Isaac

        Romans 4:19-20 tells us this about Abraham: "Being not weak in faith, he considered not his own body now dead, when he was about a hundred years old, neither yet the deadness of Sarah's womb. He staggered not at the promise of God through unbelief, but was strong in faith, giving glory to God." Even though Sarah was old and had never been able to bear children, Abraham believed God's promise that she would have a son.

Do We Really Believe God?

Professing to believe what God has said is much easier than really trusting Him. For instance, many people who affirm that "God shall supply all your need according to his riches" (Phil. 4:19) become filled with anxiety when financial trouble comes. When they panic, others say, "Aren't you the one who goes around saying 'God shall supply all your needs'?" You either believe He will or you don't, regardless of what you say. Your actions reveal what you really believe. If you worry, you are doubting that God can keep His promises, and that dishonors Him.

The Bible also says that if we give sacrificially with the proper motives, God will reward us (cf. Matt. 6:3-4). We say we believe that principle as well, but we often find it difficult to put into practice. Also, many Christians fear death, even though God has said He will provide us with the grace we need to face it and take us to heaven afterward. To be honest, most of us need to admit that we don't believe God as much as we claim.

b) The offering of Isaac

When the promised son had grown to a young boy, God told Abraham to kill him as a sacrifice. So Abraham went up a mountain with Isaac, whom he laid on an altar and tied down. He took out a knife and was ready to plunge it into Isaac's heart, but the Angel of the Lord stopped him and God provided a ram as a substitute offering (Gen. 22:1-13). Abraham obeyed because he was confident that God would provide. He could have said, "God, how can you possibly fulfill your covenant with me (with descendants numbering as the stars of heaven) if I'm going to kill the only possible fulfillment?" But Abraham didn't argue. He believed God would keep His word, even if his son was killed. According to Hebrews 11:19, Abraham believed that God could raise Isaac from the dead.

Believing God means we acknowledge His glory, which is the sum of all His attributes and the fullness of all His majesty. If He is who He says He is, then He is to be believed. You will grow spiritually when you say to God, "If Your Word says it, I will believe it; if Your Word promises it, I will claim it; and if Your Word commands it, I will obey it."

2. Shadrach, Meshach, and Abednego

   a) The test of faith

   Daniel 3:13 says, "Nebuchadnezzar in his rage and fury commanded to bring Shadrach, Meshach, and Abednego. Then they brought these men before the king." Nebuchadnezzar was angry because those young Jewish men would not worship the image he had made of himself. They would worship only the true God. In verses 14-15 he says, "Is it true, O Shadrach, Meshach, and Abednego, do not ye serve my gods, nor worship the golden image which I have set up? Now, if ye be ready . . . to fall down and worship the image which I have made, well; but if ye worship not, ye shall be cast the same hour into the midst of a burning fiery furnace. And who is that God, that shall deliver you out of my hands?" Nebuchadnezzar put their faith to the test. Did they believe their God could handle Nebuchadnezzar? They couldn't see their God, but they could see Nebuchadnezzar. They couldn't see the hosts of their God, but they could see the formidable army of Nebuchadnezzar.

   b) The testimony of faith

   Shadrach, Meshach, and Abednego replied, "O Nebuchadnezzar, we are not careful to answer thee in this matter. If it be so, our God, whom we serve, is able to deliver us from the burning fiery furnace, and he will deliver us out of thine hand, O king. But if not, be it known unto thee, O king, that we will not serve thy gods, nor worship the golden image which thou hast set up" (vv. 16-18). They knew God would deliver them—if not out of the fire, then to His righteous kingdom—because they remained true to Him.

c) The triumph of faith

Verse 19 says, "Then was Nebuchadnezzar full of fury, and the form of his visage was changed. . . . He spoke, and commanded that they should heat the furnace seven times more than it was usually heated." The men who put the young men into the furnace were burned to death because it was so hot (vv. 22-23). Shadrach, Meshach, and Abednego really did believe God. There was no human way to escape their predicament, but true faith knows no impossibilities. In their case, God provided a miraculous deliverance (vv. 24-28).

3. Noah

Noah experienced what was perhaps the greatest challenge to faith in human history (Gen. 6:14-22). God told him to build a massive boat (about the size of the *Queen Mary*) in a land that was probably a desert. It's likely he had to chop down the trees and hew the planks himself. He spent 120 years building the boat (Gen. 6:3), and everyone probably laughed at him the whole time. (It is doubtful that pre-Flood man had ever seen rain.)

To say Noah was a man of great faith is an understatement. Hebrews 11:7 says, "By faith Noah, being warned of God of things not seen as yet, moved with fear, prepared an ark to the saving of his house, by which he condemned the world, and became heir of the righteousness which is by faith." Noah's 120 years of great faith glorified God.

B. Growing by Faith

Exercising faith causes us to grow spiritually because it glorifies God. Second Corinthians 5:7 says, "We walk by faith, not by sight." That walk is our Christian progress toward the image of Christ. It takes place when we live by faith. When we judge everything by what we see, however, we will have difficulty growing. Remember the twelve spies

Israel sent into the land of Canaan (Num. 13)? Ten came back and said, "We don't want to go in there: we felt like grasshoppers because they're giants!" Those spies walked by sight, but Joshua and Caleb had faith, saying, "God is on our side; let's go in!" Ten didn't think God could handle the circumstances, but two knew He is bigger than any circumstance.

Do you live by faith? Are you like Abraham, who "staggered not at the promise of God through unbelief, but was strong in faith, giving glory to God" (Rom. 4:20)? If you want to grow spiritually, believe God's Word and trust Him in every situation.

V. BEARING FRUIT

In John 15 Jesus uses the analogy of a vine and its branches to describe our relationship with Him. Spiritually we are one with Him; we produce fruit as His life flows through us. Verse 8 says, "In this is My Father glorified, that ye bear much fruit." Fruitfulness glorifies God (and therefore energizes growth) because it is the evidence of His power at work in us.

All Christians Bear Fruit

Christians can be at many different levels of bearing fruit in their lives, but I don't believe there's such a thing as a fruitless Christian. Evidence of faith will exist in every believer, though it may be hard to find in some cases.

We had a peach tree in our backyard, and one year that thing went wild with fruit. We had enough peaches to feed the whole neighborhood! Another year we could find only one tiny, shriveled peach. But something was always there to prove it was a peach tree and not some other kind of tree. Some Christians can be like that, exhibiting little evidence of belonging to God—but God wants them to grow and produce much fruit for His glory.

A. The Importance of Bearing Fruit

The fruit you bear is the manifestation of your character, and the only way people will know that you are a child of

God. God wants to present Himself to the world through what He produces in you, so that His character is at stake in your fruit. He wants you to be fruitful far above what the world or the flesh can produce.

1. Titus 2:10—Paul told Titus to exhort believers to "adorn the doctrine of God." It should be evident that God is at work in our lives.

2. Romans 2:24—The apostle Paul said of Israel, "The name of God is blasphemed among the Gentiles through you." They claimed to belong to God but gave the world the wrong perception of Him. In fact, Jesus said to their leaders, "Ye are of your father the devil" (John 8:44). Their fruit was definitely not the product of God.

3. Matthew 5:16—Jesus said, "Let your light so shine before men, that they may see your good works, and glorify your Father, who is in heaven." God is glorified when we accurately represent Him through our good works.

B. Types of Spiritual Fruit

What kind of fruit brings glory to God? Philippians 1:11 says, "Being filled with the fruits of righteousness, which are by Jesus Christ, unto the glory and praise of God." Righteousness, which is doing right, is the fruit God desires in our lives. When we do right we glorify God; when we do wrong we dishonor Him. Fruit is synonymous with righteousness.

It is God who produces the fruit of righteousness within us so that He may be glorified. As Paul says in 2 Thessalonians 1:11-12, "We pray always for you, that our God would count you worthy of this calling, and fulfill all the good pleasure of his goodness, and the work of faith with power, that the name of our Lord Jesus Christ may be glorified in you."

There are two kinds of spiritual fruit.

1. Action fruit

   a) Leading others to Christ

   Paul said, "Now I would not have you ignorant, brethren, that oftentimes I purposed to come unto you (but was prevented thus far) that I might have some fruit among you also, even as among other Gentiles" (Rom. 1:13). What is the fruit he was referring to? Converts. He wanted to win people to Christ. Action fruit includes leading others to Christ. Is that a product of your life? It should be natural for a believer to lead others to Christ because one of the characteristics of life is reproduction.

   Paul said to Timothy, "The things that thou hast heard from me among many witnesses, the same commit thou to faithful men, who shall be able to teach others also" (2 Tim. 2:2). Jesus told us to go into the world and make disciples (Matt. 28:19). God wants us to display the life within us by reproducing it.

   b) Giving

   The Philippians had sent Paul a generous gift—a love offering. In Philippians 4:17 he tells them why he appreciated it: "Not because I desire a gift; but I desire fruit that may abound to your account." The greatest thing about their gift was that it was fruit they had produced.

   Because giving is a fruit, it should not have to be coerced. When you are filled with the Spirit and committed to glorifying God, you will give voluntarily and generously. Giving must come from the heart. My father often said, "You can give without loving, but you can never love without giving."

   c) Expressing thanks to God

   Hebrews 13:15 says, "Let us offer the sacrifice of praise to God continually, that is, the fruit of our lips giving thanks to his name." Saying thanks to God is fruit—another product of His work in your life.

Colossians 1:10 says, "That ye might walk worthy of the Lord unto all pleasing, being fruitful in every good work." Any good work is action fruit. It could be leading someone to Christ, giving a gift, thanking God, or some other righteous act. God wants to see us bear that kind of fruit.

2. Attitude fruit

Galatians 5:22-23 says, "The fruit of the Spirit is love, joy, peace, long-suffering, gentleness, goodness, faith, meekness, self-control." Those are all attitudes.

Which Come First: Attitudes or Actions?

Action fruit without attitude fruit is legalism, which was characteristic of the Pharisees. Many who tell others about Jesus do so with the wrong attitude—perhaps out of duty, obligation, or fear. Some people give their money grudgingly. Others follow a list of rules—they don't do this and they don't do that—but inside they want to do the opposite. They are acting in the right way, but they don't have the right attitude.

If we have the right attitude, however, the right action will follow automatically. When we yield ourselves to the Spirit, He produces love, joy, peace, long-suffering, gentleness, goodness, faith, meekness, and self-control in us. Those attitudes will then produce the right actions. Unfortunately, many people who think they are serving God are doing so with wrong attitudes. When they tell Jesus at the judgment that they did many wonderful works in His name (Matt. 7:22), He will say, "I never knew you; depart from me" (v. 23). We glorify God when we are fruitful both in our attitudes and in our actions.

How do we get the right attitudes? How do we become characterized by love, joy, peace, and patience? Galatians 5:25 says, "If we live in the Spirit, let us also walk in the Spirit." As we yield control of our lives to the

Holy Spirit, He will permeate our lives and produce the proper fruit.

VI. PRAISING GOD

I don't believe a Christian can grow unless his life is characterized by praise. In Psalm 50:23 God says, "Whoso offereth praise glorifieth me." If you want to glorify God, praise Him. That is another simple path to growth. Proud people don't praise God—they're too consumed with themselves. Humble people are in awe of Him, and praise pours from their hearts.

A. The Example of the Psalms

Praise is so much a part of God's pattern for His people that He gave them a hymnbook filled with it. The psalms are great hymns that were sung and spoken by the people of Israel. God wanted them to constantly offer Him the praise of which He is so worthy.

1. Psalm 86:9-10, 12—"All nations whom thou hast made shall come and worship before thee, O Lord, and shall glorify thy name. For thou art great, and doest wondrous things; thou art God alone. . . . I will praise thee, O Lord my God, with all my heart, and I will glorify thy name for evermore." Praising God is equated with giving Him glory.

2. Psalm 92:1-2—"It is a good thing to give thanks unto the Lord, and to sing praises unto thy name, O Most High; to show forth thy loving-kindness in the morning, and thy faithfulness every night." Praising the Lord in the morning and night sets the tone for our lives.

B. The Aspects of Praise

What exactly does it mean to praise God? Some think it is singing a song. Some think it is saying, "Praise the Lord! Hallelujah!" Some think it is waving your hands in the air. Some think it is silent prayer. What is the right answer? How do we praise the Lord? According to the Bible, true praise involves three things:

1. Reciting God's attributes

Praise expresses the character of God.

a) Illustrated in the Old Testament

Some people study the New Testament almost exclusively because it reveals many truths that were mysteries in the past. But one great reason to study the Old Testament is that it so powerfully reveals the character of God, enabling us to praise Him better.

For example, Habakkuk praised God for His character—that He is a holy, almighty, eternal, covenant-keeping God (Hab. 1:12-13)—and that praise solved a great problem in his own heart. He didn't understand why God was going to judge Israel by sending the evil Chaldeans to conquer them (Hab. 1:6-11). Habakkuk wanted God to revive and restore His people, but they had overstepped the limit of His patience.

In the middle of his confusion, Habakkuk remembered, "God is holy—He doesn't make mistakes. God is a covenant-keeping God—He doesn't break His promises. God is eternal—He is outside the flux of history." Following his praise, Habakkuk was able to say, "The just shall live by his faith" (Hab. 2:4). He felt better even though his circumstances hadn't changed. God did allow the Chaldeans to overrun Israel for a time, but Habakkuk knew his God was strong enough to handle any circumstances.

b) Applied to our lives today

Instead of worrying about problems we cannot solve, we should say, "Lord, You are bigger than history. You own everything in the entire universe. You can do anything You want to do. You love us and promise we will never be without the things we need. You said You would take care of us as You take care of the grass of the field. You have promised that Your character and power are at our disposal." That kind of praise glorifies God.

2. Reciting God's works

God's attributes are displayed in His works.

a) As practiced in the psalms

The psalms are filled with lists of the great things God has done. They praise Him for parting the Red Sea, bringing the people out of Egypt, parting the Jordan River, making the water flow from a rock, feeding Israel with manna in the wilderness, destroying Israel's enemies, making the walls of Jericho fall, and many other powerful works.

b) As practiced by Habakkuk

After reevaluating his problem, Habakkuk began to praise God for His works, trembling at the power displayed in them (Hab. 3:16). He said he would rejoice in the Lord even if everything crumbled around him (vv. 17-18). Why? Because God had proved Himself in the past. That's why the Old Testament contains such an extensive history of God's works—so that we can know how He has proved faithful.

c) As practiced today

If you have a problem facing you that you don't know how to solve, remember to praise God. Say to Him, "Lord, You are the God who put the stars and the planets into space. You are the God who formed the earth and separated the land from the sea. Then You made man and everything else that lives. Although man fell, You planned his redemption. You are the God who carved out a nation for Yourself and preserved it through history. You are the God who performed wonder after wonder for that nation. You are the God who wrote the law on tablets of stone. You are the God who enabled Your people to walk out of Egypt. You drowned Pharaoh's army. You are the God who came into this world in human form,

68

and then rose from the dead." When we praise God like that, our problems pale in comparison to all He has done. Remembering God's past performance glorifies Him and strengthens our faith.

3. Giving thanks for God's attributes and works

At the heart of praise is thanksgiving.

a) Illustrated by a leper

Luke 17 tells us that as Jesus "entered into a certain village, there met Him ten men that were lepers, who stood afar off. And they lifted up their voices, and said, Jesus, Master, have mercy on us. And when he saw them, he said unto them, Go show yourselves unto the priests" (vv. 12-14). According to Mosaic law, a leper could not return to society unless a priest verified that his disease was in remission. Verse 14 continues, "It came to pass that, as they went, they were cleansed." To be healed, they had to first take a step of faith based on what they had heard about Jesus.

"One of them, when he saw that he was healed, turned back, and with a loud voice glorified God, and fell down on his face at his feet, giving him thanks; and he was a Samaritan" (vv. 15-16). One of the men, an outcast from Jewish society, glorified God by thanking Jesus. "And Jesus, answering, said, Were there not ten cleansed? But where are the nine? There are not found that returned to give glory to God, except this stranger. And he said unto him, Arise, go thy way; thy faith hath made thee well" (vv. 17-19). Though all ten were physically healed, I believe that only the Samaritan was redeemed.

b) Illustrated by Paul

The apostle Paul said, "By the grace of God I am what I am; and his grace, which was bestowed upon me, was not in vain, but I labored more abundantly than they all; yet not I, but the grace of God which was with me" (1 Cor. 15:10). Paul was thankful for God's work of grace in his life.

Praising God gives Him glory. No matter what happens in our lives, we are to express our thanks to Him for His attributes and gracious works.

Spiritual growth is a result of glorifying God, so we will grow when our lives are filled with faith in God, spiritual fruit, and praise.

Focusing on the Facts

1. How did Abraham demonstrate his faith in God (see pp. 58-59)?
2. Why was King Nebuchadnezzar angry with Shadrach, Meshach, and Abednego (see p. 60)?
3. Why was Noah's building the ark a great display of faith (see p. 61)?
4. We walk by _____ , not by _____ (1 Cor. 5:7; see p. 61).
5. In John 15, what analogy does Jesus use to describe our relationship to Him (see p. 61)?
6. Why is bearing fruit so important? Support your answer with Scripture (see pp. 62-63).
7. Give a one-word definition of fruit (Phil. 1:11; see p. 63).
8. Differentiate between action fruits and attitude fruits, and give examples of each (see pp. 64-65).
9. What book in Scripture is a pattern for praising God (see p. 66)?
10. How did Habakkuk deal with the confusion he was experiencing (see p. 67)?
11. Why does the Old Testament contain such an extensive history of God's works (see p. 68)?
12. What did the lepers in Luke 17 have to do to be healed? Why (see p. 69)?
13. How did the Samaritan leper glorify God (see p. 69)?

Pondering the Principles

1. Author Jerry Bridges, in his book *Trusting God* (Colorado Springs: NavPress, 1988) identifies three essential truths about God we must understand if we're to fully trust Him:

- God is completely sovereign.
- God is infinite in wisdom.
- God is perfect in love.

Let's consider those truths. The first means God's power guarantees the accomplishment of His plan to the smallest detail, so He never says, "Huh?" The second means there are no facts or possibilities hidden from God, so He never says, "Oops." And the third means God always exercises His might and wisdom for the benefit of His children (Rom. 8:28), so He never says, "Sorry." God is never surprised, never makes mistakes, and always does what is best for us—making Him the most trustworthy Person in the universe.

2. Does your life bear fruit? Examine it in light of what you just learned in this chapter. First, what does your life tell others about God's character? If people's only perception of God was developed by looking at your life, what would they think of Him? Second, consider the three action fruits mentioned in the chapter (see pp. 64-65), and add some of your own to the list. How many of those fruits are present in your life? If some aren't, why not? Third, look at Paul's list of attitude fruits in Galatians 5:22-23. Are those attitudes the force behind your abstinence from sin and service for God? Make sure you are not doing right things from wrong motives.

3. List as many of God's attributes as you can think of, and then list His gracious works in your life. Finally, make a list of situations in your life that you tend to worry about. Recite God's attributes and works out loud in prayer, thanking Him for each one, and then look back at your list of problems. Like Habakkuk (see pp. 67-68), you will find your anxiety fading.

5
Obedience, Prayer, and Proclaiming the Word

Outline

Introduction and Review
I. Confessing Jesus as Lord
II. Aiming Our Lives at Glorifying God
III. Confessing Our Sins
IV. Trusting God
V. Bearing Fruit
VI. Praising God

Lesson
VII. Loving God Enough to Obey Him
   A. Christ's Confrontation of Peter
      1. The question
         a) Posed
         b) Repeated
      2. The prophecy
      3. The command
   B. Peter's Commitment to Christ
      1. As seen in his works
      2. As seen in his writings
VIII. Praying
   A. The Promise of Answered Prayer
      1. Given for God's glory
      2. Given to comfort the disciples
   B. The Prerequisite to Answered Prayer
   C. Praising God for Answered Prayer

Introduction and Review

Nothing is more important in the life of a believer than spiritual growth. It is tragic for a Christian to remain in a state of spiritual infancy, yet that happens in many cases. Churches are filled with people who are not growing spiritually. Many of them lose the same battles repeatedly, never gaining resources or being strengthened. Therefore they don't experience victory or a sense of usefulness to God. Because of the tragedy of retarded spiritual growth, it is important for us to understand the scriptural principles that can help us reach maturity.

I. CONFESSING JESUS AS LORD (see pp. 25-29)

Philippians 2:11 says, "Every tongue should confess that Jesus Christ is Lord, to the glory of God, the Father." The first step in glorifying God, and therefore in growing, is to confess Jesus as Lord. You cannot live to the glory of God unless you are a believer. The purpose of the new birth is not primarily to keep you out of hell or to allow you to experience blessing but to enable you to glorify God with your life. That is why He made you.

Unlike the heavens, the beasts of the field, and the elect angels, humans have resisted giving glory to God. Romans 1:21 says, "When they knew God, they glorified him not as God." Because of that sad truth, man lost his ability to progress spiritually. Only when we invite Christ into our lives as Savior and Master does spiritual growth begin.

II. AIMING OUR LIVES AT GLORIFYING GOD (see pp. 29-38)

First Corinthians 10:31 says, "Whether, therefore, ye eat, or drink, or whatever ye do, do all to the glory of God." Everything we do—even the most mundane things, such as eating and drinking—should be done for the purpose of glorifying God.

III. CONFESSING OUR SINS (see pp. 44-54)

IV. TRUSTING IN GOD (see pp. 58-62)

V. BEARING FRUIT (see pp. 62-66)

VI. PRAISING GOD (see pp. 66-70)

Spiritual maturity is not an instantaneous achievement. We grow steadily and constantly when we give God glory—a life-style described as "walking in the Spirit" (Gal. 5:16).

Lesson

VII. LOVING GOD ENOUGH TO OBEY HIM

If I could simplify the Christian life to one word it would be *obedience*. I don't just mean external obedience but a spirit of obedience. It's not like the little girl who defiantly continued to stand up after her father had told her many times to sit down. Finally her father said, "Sit down, or I'll spank you." She sat down but looked up and said, "I'm sitting down, but I'm standing up in my heart!" That's obeying outwardly but disobeying in the heart. The believer should have a willingness to obey.

A. Christ's Confrontation of Peter

John 21 shows that we glorify God by loving Him enough to obey Him. Before He could affirm Peter's call to the ministry, Jesus first confronted him about the issue of love.

1. The question

a) Posed

John 21:15 says, "Jesus saith to Simon Peter, Simon, son of Jonah . . . " Jesus called Peter by his old name because he was acting like his old self. Instead of waiting for Jesus to appear, he had returned to his former vocation of fishing (v. 3). Then Jesus said, "Lovest thou me more than these?" Jesus used the strongest word for love in the Greek language—*agapaō*. He was saying, "Do you really love Me, Peter? Do you love Me supremely?" "More than these" may have been a reference to the boats and nets or to the other disciples (cf. Matt. 26:33).

Peter replied, "Yea, Lord; thou knowest that I love thee." Peter didn't use *agapaō*; He used *phileō*, meaning, "I like You a lot." Perhaps he didn't want to say, "Lord, I super love You," because Jesus might then say, "He that hath my commandments, and keepeth them, he it is that loveth me" (John 14:21). Peter probably thought he couldn't claim to have *agapēo* love for Christ because he gave little evidence of it. He would have been like the man who wrote to his sweetheart, "I would cross the burning sand or swim the English Channel to be near you, and if it doesn't rain tonight I'm coming over." Peter claimed a lesser love and hoped the Lord would accept it. Apparently Jesus did, for He then said to Peter, "Feed my lambs." He wanted Peter to help build the kingdom by teaching God's people.

b) Repeated

John 21:16-17 says, "He saith to him again the second time, Simon, son of Jonah, lovest thou me? He saith unto him, Yea, Lord; thou knowest that I love thee. He saith unto him, Feed my sheep. He saith unto him the third time, Simon, son of Jonah, lovest thou me? Peter was grieved because he said unto him the third time, Lovest thou me? And he said unto him, Lord, thou knowest all things; thou knowest that I love thee." The reason Peter was grieved at the third question may have been that Christ used the word *phileō* rather than *agapeō*. Jesus was questioning whether Peter even liked Him.

Maybe our love isn't all that it could be; maybe it isn't *agapeō*—supreme love. But if it is even good, solid *phileō*, Christ will use us. He will take us where we are and build us up from there. Like Peter, however, we do have to love Him enough to obey Him.

2. The prophecy

In John 21:18-19 Jesus says to Peter, "Verily, verily, I say unto thee, When thou wast young, thou girdest thyself, and walkedst where thou wouldest; but when thou shalt be old, thou shalt stretch forth thy hands, and another shall gird thee, and carry thee where thou wouldest not. This spoke he, signifying by what death he [Peter] should glorify God." Jesus was saying, "Peter, do you really love Me? If you continue in My service and feed My people, it will cost you your life."

3. The command

Then Jesus said, "Follow Me" (v. 19). He didn't say, "Follow Me, and you'll be successful. You'll have health, wealth, and happiness." That's what the cults and much of today's so-called Christianity promise. Instead, Jesus told Peter, "Follow me, even though it will cost you your life."

Peter then looked at the apostle John and said, "Lord, and what shall this man do? Jesus saith unto him, If I will that he tarry till I come, what is that to thee?" (vv. 20-22). Jesus was saying, "If he lives until the second coming, that's none of your business." (Because of that statement, a rumor started that John was going to live until the second coming. John had to write verse 23 to correct that rumor.) Jesus then used an emphatic pronoun to repeat His command with more force, saying, "Follow thou me" (v. 22).

B. Peter's Commitment to Christ

1. As seen in his works

In Acts 2:14-47 we see that Peter preached a tremendous sermon in Jerusalem, and three thousand people were saved. In Acts 3:1-8 he healed a lame man who jumped up and danced around the Temple praising God. In Acts 4:5-21 he confronted the Sanhedrin, saying, "Neither is there salvation in any other, for there is no other name under heaven given among men, whereby we must be saved" (v. 12). He and John courageously said, "Whether it is right in the sight of God to hearken unto you more than unto God, judge ye" (v. 19). Peter was the shining light in the early church.

2. As seen in his writings

Peter's two epistles express the tremendous joy he had from being called into Christ's service. In 2 Peter 1:14-15 he says, "Knowing that shortly I must put off this my tabernacle, even as our Lord Jesus Christ hath shown me. Moreover, I will endeavor that ye may be able, after my decease, to have these things always in remembrance." Peter wanted to serve Christ until he died.

One evidence of spiritual maturity is loving God enough to obey Him, even when it is difficult. God is glorified when we willingly obey Him no matter what the cost. Each time we obey we grow spiritually, and each time we disobey our growth is retarded.

VIII. PRAYING

Prayer glorifies God, making it a vital element of spiritual growth.

A. The Promise of Answered Prayer

In John 14:13 Jesus says, "Whatever ye shall ask in my name, that will I do." Verse 14 repeats that great promise: "If ye shall ask anything in my name, I will do it."

1. Given for God's glory

Why does God answer prayer? Jesus gives us the primary reason at the end of verse 13: "that the Father may be glorified in the Son." God answers prayer for His sake as well as ours. He does it to put Himself on display. Understanding that increases our confidence in prayer: we can know God will answer because it is an opportunity for Him to receive glory. We will grow spiritually as we interact with God through prayer and see His power on display.

2. Given to comfort the disciples

The context of verse 13 shows that the disciples were greatly distressed because Jesus told them He would be leaving. He said, "If I go and prepare a place for you, I will come again, and receive you unto myself" (John 14:3). The disciples had relied on Jesus for so long that they feared being without Him. He had provided all their resources. He provided tax money from the mouth of a fish (Matt. 17:27) and created food when they were hungry (Matt. 14:19-21). He was their beloved friend and their spiritual, theological, and economic resource. He was their future as well as their present. So they panicked at the thought of His leaving. But He left them with a tremendous promise, saying, "Don't worry. Even though I am going, you will still have resources. Whatever you need and ask for in My name, I will do. I don't have to physically be here."

B. The Prerequisite to Answered Prayer

Praying in Jesus' name is more than a formula. Some people think that at the end of every prayer you have to say, "In Jesus' name, amen." They think results are guaranteed when you say that phrase and that the prayer doesn't get past the ceiling when you don't. But the proper kind of prayer involves much more than a formula.

What does it mean to pray in Jesus' name? In Scripture, the name of God embodies all that He is. When God told

Moses His name, He said, "I am that I am" (Ex. 3:14). Likewise, Jesus' name embodies all that He is. Jesus was saying, "When what you ask is consistent with who I am and what My will is, I will do it." Praying in Jesus' name is praying in accord with God's will (cf. 1 John 5:14). When our requests are in line with God's sovereign plan, He will answer them and our faith will increase. Instead of saying, "In Jesus' name, amen," at the end of our prayers, perhaps we should say, "I pray this because I believe it to be the will of Christ." That would eliminate many selfish requests.

Praying to Grandma

In our prayers we should not focus on what we want to receive, like the little boy who prayed, "God bless Mommy, and God bless Daddy," and then shouted, "God, I would like a new bicycle!" When his mother said, "God isn't deaf," he said, "I know, but Grandma's in the next room, and she's hard of hearing."

To pray in Jesus' name limits our prayers. For instance, I cannot know for sure if it is God's will for a sick brother to be immediately healed. But I can pray, "God, I pray that he may be comforted, grow spiritually, and honor You in the midst of his trial. This I ask because I believe it to be the will of Jesus Christ." That request is consistent with who Christ is and what Scripture reveals about His will.

Praying in the Spirit

"Praying in the Spirit" (Eph. 6:18) is not falling down and talking in some foreign language or ecstatic tongue; it is praying in a manner consistent with the will of God. Romans 8:26 says, "We know not what we should pray for as we ought; but the Spirit himself maketh intercession for us with groanings which cannot be uttered." The Spirit prays to the Father for us in a nonverbal language. His prayers are always answered because He knows the mind of the Father and prays "according to the will of God" (v. 27). Therefore, to pray in the Spirit, we must align our requests with the will of God as revealed in the Bible.

C. Praising God for Answered Prayer

When God answers our prayers about a particular situation, we have the privilege of being a part of His work and of praising Him for it. When we don't participate through prayer, we miss the opportunity to give Him glory.

Suppose someone came to a prayer meeting and said, "I had the most wonderful thing happen: The lady I've been witnessing to has opened her heart to Christ. She is now a believer and is here with us tonight. Thank you for praying for her these last few months." When that happens, someone usually says, "Praise the Lord!" and many faces turn to smiles. Those smiling would be the ones who were praying for her. But there would also be some blank, indifferent faces belonging to those who were not involved. We need to be in on what God is doing, so we can praise Him.

A Spiral Prayer List

One day a man in our church said to me, "John, I would like to pray for you, but I don't know what to pray for. Would you give me three requests?" I agreed, so he opened a little spiral notebook and wrote down each of my requests. About two weeks later he approached me and said, "John, I would like to check on those three requests." He flipped back a few pages to where he had written them and asked me what had happened in each case. I told him, and he wrote what I said in another column. So he had a request on one side and an answer on the other. When I visited his house, I noticed that he had thirteen of those spiral notebooks already filled, and was working on number fourteen! That man had seen God work.

The primary issue in prayer is not obtaining what we want but allowing God to display His glory. If we receive what we want residually, that's great, but our concern needs to be that He will do what glorifies Him most. When we pray with that attitude, we will grow spiritually, and the more faithful we are in prayer, the faster we will grow. Our faith in God's power will increase as we see Him work.

IX. PROCLAIMING GOD'S WORD

A. The Passages

1. 2 Thessalonians 3:1—"Brethren, pray for us, that the word of the Lord may have free course, and be glorified." The Word of the Lord and God Himself are synonymous in this passage. In the Old Testament, God revealed His Word Himself; in the New Testament He did so through the living Christ. God is glorified when His Word is proclaimed.

2. Galatians 1:22-24—Paul, speaking of his conversion and subsequent ministry, said, "The churches of Judaea . . . had heard only, He who persecuted us in times past now preacheth the faith which once he destroyed." The churches had heard that Saul of Tarsus, who once persecuted the faith, was now actually preaching the faith. Verse 24 says, "They glorified God [because of] me."

   To proclaim God's Word is to acknowledge it as the truth. It is a life-giving, life-changing, life-transforming, and life-sustaining Word. It is living, powerful, and sharper than a two-edged sword (Heb. 4:12). We glorify God by proclaiming His Word as the absolute source of truth.

3. Acts 13:48-49—When the Gentiles heard that salvation was available to them, "they were glad, and glorified the word of the Lord; and as many as were ordained to eternal life believed. And the word of the Lord was published throughout all the region."

B. The Process

1. Taking it in

   Spiritual growth cannot take place without the intake of God's Word. We can't grow without food, and feeding should be a daily process. To go to church on Sunday, take in a message, and hope it is enough for the whole week is like eating dinner on Sunday and saying, "Lord, that was a wonderful dinner. We pray it will hold us until next Sunday." You need to eat on Sunday, Monday, Tuesday, and so on. The same is true spiritually: there must be a daily feeding on the Word of God for optimum growth.

2. Giving it out

There is even greater glory in giving out the Word than in feeding on it. As we proclaim the Word, we cement it in our lives. In that case, the saying "The more you give away, the more you keep" is true. I have found that I tend to remember the things I teach to others but forget the things I read and never pass on.

C. The Priority

The servant of God is to give high priority to proclaiming the Word of God. When you are silent about His Word, you will retard your spiritual growth.

1. In the Old Testament

Concerning His commandments, God said, "Thou shalt teach them diligently unto thy children, and shalt talk of them when thou sittest in thine house, and when thou walkest by the way, and when thou liest down, and when thou risest up. And thou shalt bind them for a sign upon thine hand, and they shall be as frontlets between thine eyes. And thou shalt write them upon the posts of thy house, and on thy gates" (Deut. 6:7-9) The Word should so fill your heart and mind that whenever you open your mouth, its truth comes out.

Saturated in the Word

H. Clay Trumbull was a great soul winner. He said that the thing that made the difference in his life was when he determined to introduce Jesus as the topic of conversation at every opportunity (H. Clay Trumbull, *Individual Work for Individuals* [New York: YMCA,

1902], p. 23). He apparently kept that vow throughout his life by saturating himself with God's Word.

I have spent so many years studying and preaching the Bible that I would probably recite Bible verses or preach a sermon if you woke me in the middle of the night! I even dream about spiritual things; they are the context of my thinking. I thank God for putting me in a position where I can study His Word so much. To do a good job teaching the Bible, you need to saturate yourself with it. You can't just write notes and fire off a sermon; the Bible has to become a part of you so that it controls your life.

Some Unlikely Preachers

God has used some unlikely instruments to proclaim His Word: He enabled a donkey to speak to the disobedient prophet Balaam (Num. 22:28-30). Ezra 1:1 says that "the Lord stirred up the spirit of Cyrus, king of Persia" (a pagan) to make a prophecy-fulfilling proclamation. And the evil high priest Caiaphas, who helped plot Christ's death, "prophesied that Jesus should die" under divine influence (John 11:49-51).

2. In the New Testament

   a) 2 Timothy 3:16-17—"All scripture is given by inspiration of God, and is profitable for doctrine, for reproof, for correction, for instruction in righteousness, that the man of God may be perfect, thoroughly furnished unto all good works." The goal of spiritual growth is perfection. Toward that end the Bible provides doctrine, reproof, correction, and instruction in righteousness. When we are teaching, preaching, or sharing the Word of God, it takes root in our lives and energizes our growth.

   b) 2 Timothy 2:15—"Study to show thyself approved unto God, a workman that needeth not to be ashamed, rightly dividing the word of truth." The phrase "rightly dividing" literally means "cutting it straight." Paul may have been using an analogy from his profession as a tentmaker. He made his tents by cutting patterns out of goatskin. One goat was never big enough for a tent, so the skins had to be sewn together. If the individual pieces weren't cut correctly, the pattern didn't match. So Paul was saying that unless you are careful with the individual parts of Scripture, the whole will not come together.

We are to be students of the Word, filling our hearts with it. As we proclaim it, we are to hope that "the word of the Lord may have free course, and be glorified" (2 Thess. 3:1).

We glorify God by proclaiming His Word to believers and unbelievers. As we do that and practice the other keys to spiritual growth, we will become more like Christ. However, the closer we get to God, the more failures and limitations we become aware of in our lives. So we are ever pressing toward the mark (Phil. 3:14), longing for the day when "we shall be like him, for we shall see him as he is" (1 John 3:2).

X. LEADING OTHERS TO CHRIST

Leading others to Christ and building them up in the faith is a natural outgrowth of proclaiming the Word. Paul illustrated that in his commitment to the needs of the Corinthian church. Second Corinthians 4 tells us he was "troubled on every side" (v. 8), "persecuted" (v. 9), and "always bearing about in the body the dying of the Lord Jesus" (v. 10). He repeatedly suffered and faced death for their sakes, "that the abundant grace [saving grace] might through the thanksgiving of many redound to the glory of God" (v. 15). Paul entered hostile towns and confronted people because he wanted to add voices to the thanksgiving choir. He wanted more people to know of God's grace so that they could glorify Him with their lives.

Perhaps the most productive thing a believer can do is win someone else to Christ because it doubles the potential for glorifying God.

Conclusion

Spiritual growth is simply a matter of applying scriptural principles, but we sometimes think it's experienced only by spiritual giants. I have read *The Imitation of Christ*, by fifteenth-century saint
Thomas à Kempis; I have read about mystics who knelt and prayed
for eight to ten hours and wore holes in the wood floors; I have
read about Robert Murray McCheyne, who would soil the pages of
his Bible and the wood of his pulpit with great floods of tears; and I
have read *Power Through Prayer*, by E. M. Bounds, who spent hour
after hour in prayer. As I did all that I often thought, "It's useless! I
will never reach that level." But God uses each of us in different
ways. Spiritual growth is not some mystical achievement for a se-
lect few on a higher spiritual plane. Rather, it is simply a matter of
glorifying God by confessing sin, trusting Him, bearing fruit, praising Him, obeying His Word, praying, proclaiming His Word, and
leading people to Christ. Those are the qualities you need to mature. When you focus on them, the Spirit of God will change you
into the image of Christ, from one level of glory to the next.

Focusing on the Facts

1. What word well describes the Christian life (see p. 75)?
2. What two things could Jesus have meant when He asked Peter, "Lovest thou me more than these?" (John 21:15; see p. 76)?
3. Why couldn't Peter claim to have *agapēo* love for Christ (see p.
   76)?
4. How was Jesus' call to follow Him different from what the cults
   and much of today's Christianity say (see p. 77)?
5. Name several ways in which Peter exemplified his commitment to Christ later in his life (see p. 78).
6. What is the primary reason God answers prayer (see p. 79)?
7. Interacting with God through prayer allows us to see His
   _____ on display (see p. 79).
8. What does the name of God refer to in Scripture (see pp. 79-80)?
9. What does it mean to pray in Jesus' name (see p. 80)?
10. What does "praying in the Spirit" refer to (see p. 80)?
11. Name two passages in the New Testament where "the Word of
    the Lord" is used synonymously with God Himself (see p. 82).
12. Why is there greater glory in giving out the Word than in feed-
    ing on it (see p. 83)?

13. Name four things the Bible provides for the process of spiritual growth (2 Tim. 3:16-17; see p. 84).
14. What happens the closer we get to God (see p. 85)?
15. Why did Paul endanger himself repeatedly during his ministry (see p. 85)?
16. What is perhaps the most productive way of bringing glory to God (see p. 85)?

Pondering the Principles

1. Do you genuinely love God? Is your heart filled with gratefulness and affection toward Him that produce a desire to obey (cf. John 14:21-23)? The following truths from Scripture show that those are questions of eternal significance: Christians are described in Scripture as those who love God (1 Pet. 1:8; 1 John 4:19), especially in many of the familiar promises we claim (Rom. 8:28; 1 Cor. 2:9; James 1:12). Also, Paul told the Corinthians that "if any man love God, the same is known of him" (1 Cor. 8:3), and "if any man love not the Lord Jesus Christ, let him be Anathema [accursed]" (1 Cor. 16:22).

2. Do you have a prayer list? If not, try using one—at least for a month. Each request should be consistent with God's revealed will, so write down some related verses next to each one and include them in your prayer. (For example: "Lord, accomplish much through the Sunday school lesson I teach, for You've said in Isaiah 55:11, 'My word . . . shall not return unto me void . . . and it shall prosper in the thing whereto I sent it.'") Also, write down the answers to your prayers in another column, and praise God for each of them as you see Him work.

3. Taking in the Word of God without giving it out can be dangerous to your spiritual health. Imagine feeding a young boy repeatedly without giving him the chance to get up and play. Eventually his obesity and atrophied muscles would render him incapable of normal activity. Also, the boy would grow tired of the food and resentful toward those who fed him. The believer who is regularly being taught yet does not proclaim the Word can be like that young boy—overfed and unhealthy. Do you give out as much as you take in? If not, pray for opportunities to share what you learn, and make use of them.

6
Purity, Unity, and Using Our Spiritual Gifts

Outline

Review
 I. Confessing Jesus as Lord
 II. Aiming Our Lives at Glorifying God
 III. Confessing Our Sins
 IV. Trusting God
 V. Bearing Fruit
 VI. Praising God
 VII. Loving God Enough to Obey Him
VIII. Praying
 IX. Proclaiming God's Word
 X. Leading Others to Christ

Lesson
 XI. Maintaining Moral Purity
   A. Sexual Sin Is Harmful
     1. Illustrated in Proverbs
     2. Illustrated by the Israelites
     3. Illustrated by David
     4. Illustrated by Hophni and Phinehas
   B. Sexual Sin Is Enslaving
   C. Sexual Sin Is a Perversion
     1. Our body is for the Lord
     2. Our body is one with Christ
     3. Our body is a temple
XII. Preserving Unity
   A. By Receiving One Another
   B. By Being Accountable to One Another
   C. By Eliminating Division

XIII. Using Our Spiritual Gifts

Conclusion
A. The Command
B. The Result
C. The Goal

Review

We have seen that spiritual growth is not an instantaneous occurrence but a lifelong process that takes place when we glorify God. So far we have studied ten practical ways in which we can grow spiritually:

I. CONFESSING JESUS AS LORD (see pp. 25-29)

II. AIMING OUR LIVES AT GLORIFYING GOD (see pp. 29-38)

III. CONFESSING OUR SINS (see pp. 44-54)

IV. TRUSTING GOD (see pp. 58-62)

V. BEARING FRUIT (see pp. 62-66)

VI. PRAISING GOD (see pp. 66-70)

VII. LOVING GOD ENOUGH TO OBEY HIM (see pp. 75-78)

VIII. PRAYING (see pp. 78-81)

IX. PROCLAIMING GOD'S WORD (see pp. 82-85)

X. LEADING OTHERS TO CHRIST (see pp. 85-86)

Lesson

XI. MAINTAINING MORAL PURITY

You cannot grow spiritually while embracing an impure lifestyle. First Corinthians 6:19-20 says, "Know ye not that your

90

body is the temple of the Holy Spirit who is in you, whom ye have of God, and ye are not your own? For ye are bought with a price; therefore, glorify God in your body and in your spirit, which are God's." In that passage Paul was discussing moral purity, a topic relevant to our amoral society. Today's permissiveness has affected even the church, which is growing increasingly tolerant of sin—particularly sexual sin.

In 1 Corinthians 6:13 Paul says, "The body is not for fornication, but for the Lord." The Greek word translated "fornication" is *porneia*, from which we get the English word *pornography*. Its meaning includes all forms of sexual sin. In 1 Corinthians 6 Paul gives three reasons for avoiding fornication: it is harmful, it is enslaving, and it is a perversion.

A. Sexual Sin Is Harmful

Paul began by saying, "All things are lawful unto me, but all things are not expedient" (1 Cor. 6:12). The Greek word translated "expedient" (*sumpherō*) means "to be profitable." One thing it described was the pay or booty of soldiers. Paul was saying that we need to determine whether a certain activity is profitable for us.

The English word *expedient* contains the Latin word *ped*, which means "feet." *Expedient* means keeping our feet free from any entanglement. Something that is not expedient, therefore, would hinder us on our spiritual journey by tangling up our feet. Immorality is one such thing. It never helps but only harms. First Corinthians 6:18 says, "Flee fornication . . . [because] he that committeth fornication sinneth against his own body."

1. Illustrated in Proverbs

Proverbs 5-7 and 9 contain extensive lists of the devastating physical, emotional, and spiritual consequences of illicit sex.

2. Illustrated by the Israelites

First Corinthians 10:8 says, "Neither let us commit fornication, as some of them committed, and [died] in one day three and twenty thousand" (cf. Num. 25:1-9).

91

3. Illustrated by David

David's adultery with Bathsheba led to other sin and eventually left him racked with guilt. When he wrote Psalm 38, he was desperately alone and physically sick as a result of his sin.

4. Illustrated by Hophni and Phinehas

Hophni and Phinehas were the sons of Eli, the high priest. They led debauched lives even though members of the priestly line were expected to uphold high moral standards. Among other things, they "lay with the women who assembled at the door of the tabernacle" (1 Sam. 2:22). Because of their sins, God killed them (1 Sam. 2:25, 34; 4:11).

Sexual sin has terrible consequences and must be avoided. Hebrews 13:4 says, "Marriage is honorable in all, and the bed undefiled, but fornicators and adulterers God will judge."

B. Sexual Sin Is Enslaving

In 1 Corinthians 6:12 Paul says, "All things are lawful unto me, . . . but I will not be brought under the power of any." The sin of fornication, like all other sin, enslaves. I was told of a person who came to our church Sunday morning for the sermon and then went to pornographic movies in the afternoon because he couldn't free himself from that terrible lust. The more you give in to sexual sin, the more it controls you. That's why Paul determined beforehand not to do anything that would enslave him.

C. Sexual Sin Is a Perversion

Our bodies have three distinct purposes that become perverted by sexual sin.

1. Our body is for the Lord

First Corinthians 6:13-14 says, "Foods for the body, and the body for foods; but God shall destroy both it and them. Now the body is not for fornication, but for

92

the Lord; and the Lord for the body. And God hath both raised up the Lord, and will also raise us up by his own power."

The Corinthians apparently used the phrase "Foods for the body, and the body for foods" as a slogan to justify fornication. They were implying that indiscriminate sex was a necessary natural function, just like eating. We often hear the same thing today. People say, "Why do you get upset about sex? We are all sexual beings. We should express ourselves. We eat, drink, sleep, walk, and run when we want to. Why not have sex when we want to? It's biological." Paul says God has far greater purposes for our bodies than food or sex, which are both temporary because God will eventually destroy them (v. 13). Our bodies are for the Lord; He has redeemed them for resurrection and glorification. Why adulterate the special purpose God has for our bodies?

2. Our body is one with Christ

In verses 15-17 Paul says, "Know ye not that your bodies are the members of Christ? Shall I, then, take the members of Christ, and make them the members of an harlot? God forbid [Gk., *mē genoito*—the strongest negative in the Greek language]. What? Know ye not that he who is joined to an harlot is one body? For two, saith he, shall be one flesh. But he that is joined unto the Lord is one spirit." When a Christian joins with a prostitute, he is involving Christ (with whom he is one) in that vile relationship. Verse 18 says, "Flee fornication. Every sin that a man doeth is outside the body; but he that committeth fornication sinneth against his own body." Sexual sin damages our bodies, which are "members of Christ" (v. 15).

3. Our body is a temple

Verses 19-20 says, "Know ye not that your body is the temple of the Holy Spirit who is in you, whom ye have of God, and ye are not your own? For ye are bought with a price." We should not be involved in fornication because the Holy Spirit dwells in us.

We find the key to moral purity in verse 20: "Therefore, glorify God in your body and in your spirit." From time to time I meet people involved in an adulterous relationship who are convinced they have God's blessing. "The Lord brought us together," they say. But that is impossible: no one living in a state of immorality can glorify God. To grow spiritually we must be morally pure.

XII. PRESERVING UNITY

We grow faster when we don't have to grow alone. Hebrews 10:24 says, "Let us consider one another to provoke unto love and to good works." All of us in the Body of Christ have received spiritual gifts, so we can minister to each other and stimulate growth. Therefore God is glorified in the unity of the saints. Romans 15:5-6 says, "The God of patience and consolation grant you to be likeminded one toward another according to Christ Jesus, that ye may with one mind and one mouth glorify God." God doesn't expect us to struggle along the path of spiritual growth alone.

A. By Receiving One Another

Romans 15:7 says, "Receive ye one another, as Christ also received us to the glory of God." Paul was saying, "Don't exclude anyone. Christ accepted us; do we have a higher standard for our group than He does?" Christians desperately need to interact with one another; no one grows in a vacuum.

B. By Being Accountable to One Another

I have found that the closer I am to the godly people around me, the easier it is for me to live a righteous life because they hold me accountable. If something isn't right in my life, they point it out to me. God has given me a wife and children who expect me to walk a righteous path. If I stray from it, one or sometimes all five of them will inform me that I am out of line.

It's easy for a person to say, "I'm going to live my spiritual life the best way I can without getting involved in a church or having close friends. I'm the quiet type." But that person will have a difficult time growing. Accountability applies a helpful pressure toward godliness. We need the provocation Hebrews 10:24 mentions to guide us into spiritual patterns.

C. By Eliminating Division

In 1 Corinthians 1:10 Paul says, "I beseech you, brethren, by the name of our Lord Jesus Christ, that ye all speak the same thing, and that there be no divisions among you, but that ye be perfectly joined together in the same mind and in the same judgment." In verses 11-13 he says to cut out all the contentions, factions, and cliques. He wanted them to be unified because they needed one another.

We grow better in a group than we do alone.

XIII. USING OUR SPIRITUAL GIFTS

First Peter 4:10 says, "Every man hath received the gift." All Christians are gifted by God for spiritual service. I believe each one has a unique gift (a combination of the gifts listed in Romans 12 and 1 Corinthians 12) intended to meet a particular need in the Body of Christ. We each play a strategic role as we use our gift. Therefore Peter said, "As every man hath received the gift, even so minister the same one to another, as good stewards of the manifold grace of God. If any man speak, let him speak as the oracles of God; if any man minister, let him do it as of the ability which God giveth, that God in all things may be glorified through Jesus Christ" (1 Pet. 4:10-11). So don't teach mere human wisdom if you have a speaking gift, and don't work in the flesh if you have a serving gift. When we use our gift for God's glory and not our own, we will grow spiritually.

Conclusion

We grow spiritually when we glorify God by confessing Jesus as Lord, aiming our lives at His glory, trusting Him, bearing fruit, praising Him, lovingly obeying Him, praying, proclaiming His Word, maintaining moral purity, preserving unity, and using our spiritual gifts.

A. The Command

Second Peter 3:18 says, "Grow in grace, and in the knowledge of our Lord and Savior, Jesus Christ." That's a command. Your reply is either yes or no. When you say, "Yes, Lord, I want to mature," you will experience blessing, usefulness, and victory by following the biblical path of glorifying God.

B. The Result

In Psalm 16:8-9 David says, "I have set the Lord always before me. . . . Therefore my heart is glad." Spiritual maturity produces joy. According to Ephesians 2:7 God will pour out His kindness on us throughout all eternity. He wants our entire life to be characterized by joy and contentment, but that can happen only when we are growing spiritually.

C. The Goal

The apostle John summed up the goal of spiritual growth: "Beloved, now are we the children of God, and it doth not yet appear what we shall be, but we know that, when he shall appear, we shall be like him; for we shall see him as he is" (1 John 3:2). The growth process will end the day we see Jesus Christ and become like Him. Until then, "Every man that hath this hope in him purifieth himself" (1 John 3:3).

Focusing on the Facts

1. Define fornication. What are three reasons for avoiding it (see p. 91)?
2. Give some examples from the Old Testament of the harmful consequences of sexual sin (see pp. 91-92).
3. What slogan did the Corinthians apparently use to justify fornication? What does it mean (see p. 93)?
4. Whom does a Christian involve when he joins with a prostitute (see p. 93)?
5. What is the difference between fornication and every other sin, according to 1 Corinthians 6:18 (see p. 93)?

6. Who dwells in the believer's body (1 Cor. 6:19-20; see p. 93)?
7. What are we to provoke one another to (Heb. 10:24, see p. 94)?
8. Name three ways we can preserve unity (see pp. 94-95).
9. How many Christians are gifted by God for spiritual service (1 Pet. 4:10-11; see p. 95)?
10. What is the result of spiritual growth (see p. 96)?
11. What is the goal of spiritual growth (see p. 96)?

Pondering the Principles

1. Sexual sin has effects far beyond the physical realm. C. S. Lewis wrote, "Whenever a man lies with a woman, there, whether they like it or not, a transcendental relation is set up between them which must be eternally enjoyed or eternally endured" (*The Screwtape Letters* [New York: Macmillan, 1959], p. 83). Sexual intimacy is the deepest uniting of two persons (cf. 1 Cor. 6:16), so the abuse of it corrupts us at the deepest level. Let that be a sober reminder when facing temptation, and an encouragement to flee compromising situations.

2. Because we are more prone to sin when we think no one else is involved, accountability is one of the most effective ways to overcome temptation. If you are struggling with a particular sin, confess it to someone and ask him or her to check up on you regularly. Be honest when you have failed, remembering that "two are better than one . . . for if they fall, the one will lift up his fellow. But woe to him that is alone when he falleth; for he hath not another to help him up" (Eccles. 4:9-10).

Scripture Index

Topical Index